COOKING
HAWAIIAN
STYLE

COOKING HAWAIIAN STYLE

'Ohana Recipes
from Lanai & Friends

BY LANAI **TABURA** & FRANK **ABRAHAM**

COOKING
HAWAIIAN STYLE
The Art of Island Cuisine ✳

Mutual Publishing

Library of Congress Control Number: 2014947155

ISBN: 978-1939487-41-4

www.CookingHawaiianStyle.com
All recipes © by each contributor
Food photography © Leigh Anne Meeks
Studio photography © Ryan Sakamoto
Design by Courtney Tomasu

First Printing, October 2014

Mutual Publishing, LLC
1215 Center Street, Suite 210
Honolulu, Hawai'i 96816
Ph: 808-732-1709 / Fax: 808-734-4094
email: info@mutualpublishing.com
www.mutualpublishing.com

Printed in South Korea

CONTENTS

Foreword ix

Introduction xi

CHAPTER 1
KEEP IT SIMPLE

RADASHA HO'OHULI'S
Pork & Beans with Hot Dogs ... 2

AUGIE T'S
Corned Beef & Cabbage 3

MAHEALANI RICHARDSON'S
Oscar The Grouch
Applesauce 4

MAHEALANI RICHARDSON'S
Swamp Juice 4

DAVID RYUSAKI'S
Tater Tot Casserole 5

CAROLINE HOKE'S
(CAROLINE'S CREATIONS)
Parmesan Garlic Wings 6

CAROLINE HOKE'S
Kim Chee Edamame 7

MALIKA DUDLEY'S
Couscous 8

LANAI TABURA'S
Crescent Roll Lasagna 10

LANAI TABURA'S
Hamburger Broccoli 10

SID ALAPAI'S
Macadamia Nut Hummus 11

FRANK ABRAHAM'S
Kamaboko Omelette 12

AMY KRISTY'S
Spam Quiche 13

CHAPTER 2
PLATE LUNCH
FAVORITES

AUNTY BEA RODRIGUES'
Pastele Stew 16

ELENA'S RESTAURANT
Sari Sari 18

TITUS CHAN'S
Pork Chow Mein
(Gravy Noodles) 21

RAIATEA HELMS'
Kahuku Style Garlic Shimp 22

RAIATEA HELMS'
Chicken Lū'au Stew 24

MOM TABURA'S
Spaghettini Crab Salad 25

CHRIS SOUZA'S
Okazuya-Style Chow Fun 26

FRANK ABRAHAM'S
Crispy Gau Gee (Wontons) 27

SUGOI'S HAWAI'I
Garlic Furikake Chicken 28

SUGOI'S HAWAI'I
Teri Loco Moco 29

DEIRDRE TODD'S
Hanamā'ulu-Style Shrimp 30

DEIRDRE TODD'S
Mai Tai Soo
(Chop Suey Cake) 31

FRANK ABRAHAM'S
Killer Brown Gravy 32

FRANK ABRAHAM'S
Hamburger Curry 33

FRANK ABRAHAM'S
Chinese Roast Style
Fried Chicken 34

SENATOR DANIEL INOUYE'S
Sweet & Sour Spare Ribs 35

CHEF IPPY AIONA'S
Pork Belly Adobo 36

CHEF IPPY AIONA'S
Beef Steak Tataki 39

CHAPTER 3
BACK TO OUR ROOTS

DANIEL ANTHONY'S
Instant Pa'i 'ai Kulolo 42

DANIEL ANTHONY'S
Koena Meatloaf 43

KALEO PILANCA'S
Hamburger Watercress with
Chomorro Ribs & Finadene
Sauce 44

COLLEEN HANABUSA'S
Fresh 'Ahi Pasta 46

COLLEEN HANABUSA'S
Clam Pasta 48

MELVEEN LEED'S
Crustacean Polynesia 49

POPO JUNE TONG'S
Pork Hash 50

POPO JUNE TONG'S
Shrimp Toast 51

LANAI TABURA'S MOM'S
Pinakbet 52

DEIRDRE TODD'S
Char Siu Gin Doi 53

CHAPTER 4
WITH A TWIST!

KIMI WERNER'S
Smoked 'Ahi Pizza 56

ONDA PASTA'S
Kahuku Shrimp
& Fresh Pasta 58

OLENA HEU'S
Bombucha Salad with Seared
Poke & Liliko'i Vinaigrette 60

RAYMOND NOH'S
Poke Trio 62

RAYMOND NOH'S
Kim Chee Steak 63

BETTY SHIMABUKURO'S
Ramen Burger 64

GLEN SHINSATO'S
Cured Pork Patty Sandwich .. 66

GLEN SHINSATO'S
Cured Pork Chop
with Arugula Butter 67

SID ALAPAI'S
Adobo Fried Chicken 68

FRANK ABRAHAM'S
Kālua Lū'au Lasagna Rolls
with Haupia Béchamel Sauce 69

FRANK ABRAHAM'S
Teriyaki Chicken Skewers with
Fresh Tomato Chimichurri 70

LANAI TABURA'S
Snapper Egg Foo Young 72

SAI KAIROD'S
Cilantro Chili
Chicken Skewers 73

LORI IKEDA'S
Green Onion
and Chili Oil Pa'i 'Ai Biscuits . 74

LORI IKEDA'S
Pa'i 'ai Crackers 76

KAROLYN FUJIMOTO'S
Yakisoba Egg Rolls 77

THYRA ABRAHAM'S
Stuffed Sushi Cones 79

FRANK ABRAHAM'S
Shrimp, Edamame
& Corn Tempura Fritters 80

PATRICIA ANDERSON'S
Apricot Turnovers 103

FRANK ABRAHAM'S
Taro Chip Cookies 104

BETTY SHIMABUKURO'S
Crockpot Coconut Tapioca 105

FRANK ABRAHAM'S
Kona Coffee
Macadamia Brittle 106

THYRA ABRAHAM'S
Fresh Mango & Jello
Cheesecake 107

CHAPTER 5
SWEETS

WALLY AMOS'
Perfect Chocolate Chip
Macadamia Cookies 85

HULA BABY BISCOTTI'S
Papalua Fudge Cake with Mele
Mac Coconut Swiss Meringue
Buttercream 86

FRANK ABRAHAM'S
Chinese Rice Cake 90

FRANK ABRAHAM'S
Island Princess Hawai'i Mele Mac
& Macadamia Nut Pie 91

ISLAND PRINCESS HAWAI'I
Mini Mele Peanut Butter
Cookies 92

THYRA ABRAHAM'S
Chocolate Haupia Pie 94

MALIKA DUDLEY'S
Macadamia Nut Crêpes 97

THYRA ABRAHAM'S
Liliko'i Chiffon Pie 98

LORI IKEDA'S
Guava Cream Cheese
Custard Rolls 100

CHRIS SOUZA'S
Crisp Coconut Cookies 102

CHAPTER 6
CHEFS' SPECIALS

CHEF NICOLE LATORRE'S
'Ahi Carpaccio 110

CHEF ADAM TABURA'S
Steamed 'Ōpakapaka 113

CHEF ADAM TABURA'S
'Ōpakapaka Sashimi 114

CHEF ADAM TABURA'S
'Ōpakapaka Soup 117

CHEF ADAM TABURA'S
Braised Beef Brisket
Loco Moco 118

CHEF MAVRO'S
Salt Crusted Onaga
with Fresh Ogo Sauce 121

Glossary 124

Recipe Index 125

Index 127

About the Authors 130

FOREWORD

You can't be shy and a reporter at the same time. It takes a certain amount of self-possession to chase down information from strangers.

But you can be camera-shy.

Back when I decided on a career in journalism, the choice was print or broadcast. A lot of us who picked print did so because we didn't want anything to do with being in front of a camera. All these years later (never mind how many), I still would rather have dental work than be on TV.

But when I took up food writing, I started receiving offers to do cooking demos on television. Generally, I would come up with some conflict—family commitment, work commitment, anything—to get me out of it.

Then came Frank Abraham.

I managed to dodge him for the first season of *Cooking Hawaiian Style*, but then he beat me down and got me on the show in Season 2.

It was still only a little less uncomfortable than dental work, but I chalked it up as a positive experience, thanks to the combo of Frank, who did all of my prep work; Frank's mom, Thyra, who kept saying nice things; and host Lanai Tabura, one of those rare personalities who could make Scrooge McDuck look charming.

By the end of the day I had three new friends.

Frank and Lanai both love food, love eating and love Hawai'i. The sum of those parts is passion, which is clear in their commitment to this project, *Cooking Hawaiian Style*. The OC 16 show and the website

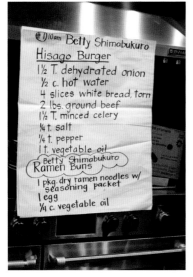

from which it originated are not just about recipes, but also the people of Hawai'i and the foods that connect us to each other and to our home.

This collection offers a taste of the show and the website. If you are already a fan, this cookbook will help you bring the dishes from the screen into your own kitchen. It also can stand alone as a diverse recipe collection, local-style, but if you let it draw you into the world of Frank and Lanai—via TV screen or computer screen—you'll probably find, as I did, that you've got a couple of new friends.

Betty Shimabukuro
Managing editor and "By Request" columnist
Honolulu Star-Advertiser

INTRODUCTION

nlike most cookbooks where one author shares his or her own recipes, this one is different. *Cooking Hawaiian Style* features recipes from all of our guests who have appeared on our cooking show as well as the website. There is a wide range of recipes from the easy-to-make Corned Beef & Cabbage to the more elegant Salt Crusted Onaga with Fresh Ogo Sauce, and everything in between. Recipes from every day people like me who love to eat and experiment, and award-winning chefs and celebrities who love to show off their flair for cooking. Many of these recipes have been handed down from generation to generation, family to family, and from our 'ohana to yours.

One of the main reasons for building the website and cooking show was to start documenting and preserving a vital part of our culture—our food. As people get wrapped up in this fast-paced, technology-driven world, I feel we are losing touch with our selves, our culture, and community. We are seeing it everyday as some of our most cherished restaurants and businesses close because the next-of-kin isn't interested in carrying on the family business.

My hope is that the pictures, recipes, stories and notes about each contributor will re-ignite fond memories of growing up in Hawai'i, will remind you of some of your favorite foods, or will inspire you to continue *Cooking Hawaiian Style*.

COOKING HAWAIIAN STYLE

CHAPTER 1

KEEP IT SIMPLE

Radasha Hoʻohuli's
Pork & Beans with Hot Dogs

Radasha Hoʻohuli, Miss Hawaiʻi 2006, hails from the west side—Nānākuli. I've been friends with Radasha for about 15 years now. I first met her when she was dancing in the Paradise Cove lūʻau show. This girl can dance! I asked her if she could come on the show and cook for us. She said, "I don't cook!" I asked her to come on and make something she grew up eating or considered comfort food. After bugging her a few more times she agreed to join *Cooking Hawaiian Style* and made one of her favorites and mine, Pork & Beans with Hot Dogs.

– Lanai Tabura

1 package hot dogs
1 tablespoon oil
1/2 round onion, slivered
2 cans pork & beans
1/2 cup brown sugar

Boil hot dogs in a small pot with 1/4 cup of water for about 5 minutes. Remove hot dogs from pot and cut diagonally into 1-inch pieces and set aside. Heat a pan with 1 tablespoon of oil on medium-high heat. Add onions and cook for 2 to 3 minutes. Add hot dogs and cook for another 2 to 3 minutes. Add pork and beans and brown sugar to pan. Reduce heat to medium. Cook covered for 10 minutes and serve!

AUGIE T'S CORNED BEEF & CABBAGE

Augie Tulba has been part of Hawai'i's landscape of entertainers for the past 20 years. Opening for comedians like Damon Wayons and Howie Mandel, he is one of Hawai'i's funniest. I was first introduced to Augie by Andy Bumatai at a fashion show I was hosting. Andy said, " Hey I got this new comedian from Kalihi. You can give him 5 minutes?" That was about 20 years ago and we have been friends since. When he's not making people laugh or working in front of the camera Augie enjoys cooking. One of his favorites is corn beef and cabbage. If you are from Hawai'i this is one of those classics that you just have to have every once in a while.

– Lanai Tabura

1 can corned beef
1 head cabbage, chopped
Salt & pepper to taste
1 tablespoon Aloha Shoyu (soy sauce)
1 tablespoon oyster sauce

Heat pan and add corned beef. Once the fat in the corned beef starts to melt, use your cooking spoon to break up the corned beef. Add one tablespoon of oil if your corned beef is dry. Add cabbage to the corned beef. Stir and cook for about 10 minutes. Sometimes adding a tablespoon of water helps create more steam, allowing the cabbage to cook faster. Season with salt, pepper, shoyu and oyster sauce. Cook for a few more minutes until the cabbage is cooked, but still has a little bit of crunch.

MAHEALANI RICHARDSON'S
OSCAR THE GROUCH APPLESAUCE

Former news anchor Mahealani Richardson visited us at the Ferguson Kitchen bringing us great ideas for infusing nutrition into foods that children will love. I have known Mahea and her husband for some time now and she always has a great happy vibe. Being a mommy she decided to share some recipes for the keiki.

-Lanai Tabura

10 apples (Gala or other sweet type with greener skin color), halved
1/2 cup water
Small bunch kale, chopped

Put apples in pot with water and cook on medium-high heat until tender (about 10 minutes). Turn heat off and add kale to cooked apples. Put mixture in blender or use an immersion blender and blend until desired consistency is achieved. Chill before serving.

MAHEALANI RICHARDSON'S SWAMP JUICE

6 to 8 ounces apple juice
1 banana
Small handful of spinach

Add all ingredients into blender. Add ice if you prefer and blend. Simple!

DAVID RYUSAKI'S TATER TOT CASSEROLE

I am constantly searching the internet for potential recipe contributors and occasionally I will place ads looking for people with interesting recipes. David responded to an ad that I placed on Craigslist and became a regular contributor to the website. This recipe quickly became one of the top recipes.

– Frank Abraham

1 pound ground beef
2 eggs
2 slices bread, broken into pieces
1/3 cup milk
1 round onion, chopped
Dash of salt and pepper
2 tablespoons dry onion soup mix
1 can cream of mushroom soup
1 can cream of chicken soup
1 cup frozen peas (optional)
1 cup shredded cheddar cheese (optional)
1 box frozen potato tater tots

Preheat oven to 350°F. In a mixing bowl, combine ground beef, eggs, bread, milk, onion, salt and pepper. Mix very well. Lightly press mixture evenly on the bottom of a 9 x 13-inch pan. Combine both cans of soup with the onion soup mix and peas (optional). Pour over meat. Layer the top of the casserole with cheese (optional) and top with tater tots. Bake uncovered for 40 to 45 minutes.

Caroline Hoke's (Caroline's Creations) Parmesan Garlic Wings

One day I received an email from Caroline offering to share a couple of recipes. It wasn't long before Caroline became an on-going and featured contributor to the website. She is originally from Hilo, Hawai'i and now hosts her own recipe blog (http://carolinesfoodcreations. blogspot.com) from Federal Way in Washington state.

– Frank Abraham

GARLIC PARMESAN SAUCE:

8 cloves garlic, peeled
2 tablespoons olive oil
1/2 cup mayonnaise
1 tablespoon corn syrup
2 tablespoons grated Parmesan cheese
1 teaspoon fresh lemon juice
1 tablespoon apple cider vinegar
1/4 teaspoon thyme
1/4 teaspoon marjoram
1/4 teaspoon oregano
1/4 teaspoon basil
1/2 teaspoon red pepper flakes
1/2 teaspoon salt
1/4 teaspoon black pepper

3 to 4 pounds chicken wings
Oil for frying
Flour to coat chicken

Heat oven to 350°F. Place the garlic cloves in a small baking dish and drizzle with the olive oil. Cover tightly with aluminum foil and bake 20 to 25 minutes, until garlic is tender. While the garlic is baking, add the remainder of the ingredients to a bowl and whisk until smooth. When the garlic is tender, remove from oven and allow to cool (about 5 minutes). Crush the garlic into the sauce using a garlic press or mash with the edge of a knife. Mix well. Refrigerate for a few hours or overnight.

Heat oil to 375°F. Coat wings in flour, shaking off the excess. Fry wings until golden brown (about 10 to 12 minutes). Remove from oil, drain briefly on paper towels. Put wings in a large bowl and toss with sauce; amount will vary according to your preference. Serve with dipping sauce on the side.

Caroline Hoke's Kim Chee Edamame

2 packages frozen edamame
1 tablespoon garlic salt
1 to 2 tablespoons gochujang (Korean chili sauce)
1 teaspoon sesame oil
1 teaspoon finely minced garlic

Cook soybeans according to package directions. Mix all ingredients in a gallon-sized ziplock bag. Chill in refrigerator for 1 to 2 hours before serving.

MALIKA DUDLEY'S COUSCOUS

Malika Dudley a woman of many talents: karate black belt, surfer, Miss Hawai'i and now a cook! Malika is one of my best friends and if you watch the show, you will see how much fun we have together. Over the years we have traveled and eaten a lot of food and I am excited to have her share a few of her family's recipes with you.

-Lanai Tabura

1 to 2 cups fine grain couscous
Salt to taste
1 to 2 tablespoons butter

TABBOULEH:

4 Roma tomatoes, cubed
1 cucumber, cubed (about 1 cup)
1 small red onion or scallion, sliced
    (about 1/4 cup)
1 cup rough chopped flat leaf parsley
2 cloves garlic, chopped
1 cup chopped cilantro
1 cup chopped mint
1/2 red bell pepper, cubed
1 lemon

VINAIGRETTE:

2 tablespoons French Dijon mustard
2 tablespoons red wine vinegar
1/4 cup quality olive oil
Salt & pepper to taste

Take desired amount of couscous and wash with water, drain until excess water is gone. With hands, fluff the wet couscous to add air. Let sit for 10 minutes or so. Don't be afraid to fluff again. Put steamer on stove with about one inch of water in the bottom. Bring to a boil. Put the steamer on top and add couscous (it will have absorbed all of the water). Do not pack it down, but make sure that the couscous is even in the pan. Wait until steam rises out of the top, about 5 minutes. Put a little bit of salt in a big bowl with some water, a thimble full, and remove the couscous from the heat and put into the bowl. Mix with a fork until the water is absorbed and let rest for a couple of minutes. Put steamer top back on and add couscous again. Let steam for another 10 minutes. Put butter in the bottom of the bowl, put couscous in bowl and mix butter in to taste. Couscous should be fluffy and delicious.

TABBOULEH:

Chop all ingredients into very small pieces. Add to couscous to taste.

VINAIGRETTE:

Add mustard, vinegar and oil to a small glass bowl and mix until smooth. Double the recipe for extra dressing. Add salt and pepper to taste. Add to couscous-tabbouleh mixture to taste.

LANAI TABURA'S CRESCENT ROLL LASAGNA

2 tablespoons olive oil
1/2 cup chopped onions
1 clove garlic, finely chopped
1 pound ground beef
1 small can olives
1 (8-ounce) can tomato sauce
Salt & pepper to taste
Italian seasoning (optional)
2 cups grated cheddar cheese
2 cans crescent dinner rolls

Heat skillet with olive oil. Sauté onions and garlic. Add ground beef and cook until browned. Add olives, tomato sauce, salt, pepper. Optional: add Italian seasoning to taste. Set aside to cool for 5 to 10 minutes.

In a 8 x 8-inch pan, place a layer of crescent dough on bottom. Add a layer of meat mixture, then cheese, dough, meat, cheese, dough. Bake at 375°F for about 25 minutes.

LANAI TABURA'S HAMBURGER BROCCOLI

Oil
1 to 2 cloves garlic, minced
1 pound ground beef
2 cans cream of mushroom soup
1 can water
Salt & pepper to taste
1 package broccoli florets
1/4 cup milk (optional)

Heat oil in pan or pot and cook garlic, add ground beef and cook until browned. Add cream of mushroom soup, water and season to taste. Add broccoli, stir once and simmer for 20 minutes on medium heat. Add a splash of milk (optional).

Sid Alapai's Macadamia Nut Hummus

1/2 cup roasted Island Princess Hawai'i macadamia nuts
1-1/2 cups garbanzo beans, drained
3 tablespoons macadamia nut or olive oil
3 tablespoons fresh lemon juice
3 tablespoons water
1/2 teaspoon minced garlic
10 medium basil leaves
Salt & pepper to taste
1 package taro chips

In a food processor combine all ingredients and pulse to purée. Refrigerate for 2 hours and serve as a dip with taro or pita chips. Makes 2 cups.

Frank Abraham's Kamaboko Omelette

This recipe is a tribute to Mr. Yoshino who introduced me to a kamaboko omelette at Like Like Drive Inn. I was amazed at how simple yet delicious it was.... so here's to you Mr. Yoshino....

SAUCE:

2 tablespoons butter
1 tablespoon Aloha Shoyu (soy sauce)
1 teaspoon oyster sauce

3 to 4 eggs
1 tablespoon butter
1/2 cup kamaboko, cut into strips
1/8 cup green onions, sliced
2 slices American cheese
Salt & pepper to taste
2 slices kamaboko, for garnish
Sliced green onion, for garnish

Make sauce ahead by melting butter, adding shoyu and oyster sauce. Mix well and set aside.

In a bowl, scramble eggs. Heat small frying pan and melt butter. Add kamaboko strips and green onions, cook for 30 seconds to 1 minute. Pour scrambled eggs over mixture. Cook on medium-low heat. Once eggs are 3/4 cooked,

add American cheese to middle and gently fold omelette over. Serve on dish with rice. Garnish with sauce, chopped kamaboko and green onion.

Amy Kristy's Spam Quiche

Like a lot of expats, Amy left Hawai'i to go to school in Washington and never made it back. She misses the food and constantly creates her own Hawai'i-inspired recipes as a way to stay connected. With almost 200 recipe contributions, Amy shares her take on island cuisine with all of us.

6 large eggs, beaten
1/2 cup half & half
1/4 teaspoon dry mustard
1/4 cup chopped onion
1/2 teaspoon garlic salt
1/2 teaspoon pepper
1 can spam, diced into small cubes
1 cup Cheddar cheese, shredded
1/4 cup Parmesan cheese
1 store-bought deep dish pie crust

Preheat oven to 350°F. Mix first six ingredients in a large mixing bowl. Pour mixture into pie crust. Add spam and cheese evenly into egg mixture and gently fold. Top with Parmesan cheese. Bake for 40 minutes until center is firm and a toothpick inserted in center comes out clean. Allow to rest a few minutes before slicing.

OOKING HAWAIIAN STYLE

CHAPTER 2

Plate Lunch Favorites

Aunty Bea Rodrigues' Pastele Stew

I met Aunty Bea for the first time when she was a guest on the show. She was a former Miss Puerto Rico, and when you ask her when she held her title, she says, "Long time ago!" She is one of those ladies who is everyone's aunty with a great wit and sense of humor. I am a huge fan of Pastele Stew and Aunty Bea shows us the real and authentic way to make it. Once you try this recipe, make sure you make a big pot and invite the neighbors over!

-Lanai Tabura

8 green bananas

ACHIOTE OIL:

1 cup vegetable oil
1 package achiote seeds

3 to 4 pounds pork butt, cut in cubes
Salt & pepper to taste
1 tablespoon cumin
1 tablespoon oregano
2 onions, chopped
2 bell peppers, chopped
1 clove garlic, crushed
4 to 6 Hawaiian chili peppers, chopped
2 bundles cilantro, chopped
3 cups water
1 small can tomato paste
1 small can olives, seedless and whole

MASA:

To make masa, first slice the skin of green bananas all the way down on each side lengthwise, then soak green bananas in really hot water for 5 to 10 minutes. This makes taking the skin off very easy. Peel bananas and grate using a fine grater into a bowl. Set aside.

ACHIOTE OIL:

Heat vegetable oil in old pot and add achiote seeds. Cook for 5 to 10 minutes and remove from heat. Keep oil in pot and allow to cool. You can store oil for later use in a glass jar. Use extreme caution when working with achiote oil as it will stain.

STEW:

Cook pork with vegetable oil in large pot adding salt and pepper. Add cumin and oregano. Add chopped onions, bell peppers,

(continued on page 18)

crushed garlic, chopped chili peppers and cilantro to pot and cook for 30 minutes. Add 3 cups water and cook another 45 minutes.

Taste and add additional salt/pepper and seasonings if necessary. Add tomato paste and cook another 30 minutes. Add half of the achiote oil to the stew. Stir well then add remaining oil. Add can of olives and add green banana (masa) one large spoon at a time, slowly until desired thickness is achieved.

ELENA'S RESTAURANT SARI SARI

We just had to have Richard Butuyan on our show, because one of my favorite Filipino food restaurants is Elena's. I was trying to get one of the owner's sister, Melissa, on the show as well because she is a good friend. But she wasn't having it. We were lucky to at least get one of them. Elena's is a household name in Hawai'i not only because of the restaurant but because they had one of the first food trucks. They are the oldest Filipino restaurant in Hawai'i, started by Elena and Theo Butuyan just over 40 years ago. Filipino food in Hawai'i become popular in the plantation days as the immigrants of Ilocas Norte showed up on the plantation fields. The style of food has become such a part of our local culture, I can't go a week without any Filipino food. Richard shares a very simple and healthy dish, Sari Sari.

– Lanai Tabura

1 long squash (opu)
1 long eggplant (dark purple)
1 bunch ong choi leaves (no stems)
2 round yellow onions
2 pieces ginger, minced
1 clove garlic, minced
2 medium tomatoes
1/2 pound crispy pork belly (lechon kawali), chopped into 1/2 x 2-inch pieces
Water
Patis to taste
1 pound small shrimp, peeled and deveined
Hawaiian salt to taste
1 bitter melon, sliced

Cut vegetables into bite-sized pieces. Other vegetables that can be used are long beans or green beans, and squash or chayote. Heat oil in a large heavy pot over medium-high heat. Sauté ginger, garlic and tomato in oil until garlic is translucent.

Add roast pork and stir-fry for two to three minutes until pork is heated

through. Add in vegetables (except bitter melon) and patis (start with 1 tablespoon).

Reduce heat to medium. Partially cover pot and simmer, stirring occasionally until vegetables are almost tender. Add water if necessary to prevent sticking. Add shrimp and continue cooking until shrimp are pink and done. Adjust seasoning by adding salt or additional fish sauce. Add in bitter melon. Cook until bitter melon is tender. Do not stir; shake pot instead. Do not over cook or damage bitter melon, which can be omitted if you don't like the bitter taste.

Titus Chan's
Pork Chow Mein (Gravy Noodles)

I always heard of Titus Chan but never got to meet him until he came on the show. He is what you call one of the classic, original chefs. Before the Food Network, Titus had his own cooking show, so he knew his way around a kitchen and how to work the camera. Our first meeting, before we started taping, I was a little worried because he didn't look too organized. As soon as we started rolling, he lit up and there was no need to encourage him to talk! He's a great guy and it was a pleasure meeting him and having him as a guest. His style is old school, and I love it because that's what we are missing today.

– Lanai Tabura

2 to 3 teaspoons oil
2 (12-ounce) packages chow mein noodles
1/2 pound pork, cut into pieces
1 bell pepper, cut into pieces
1 onion, cut into 1-inch pieces
2 cloves garlic, finely chopped
1 cup snow peas, washed and de-stringed

SEASONING:

2 teaspoons sherry
1-1/2 cans chicken broth (3 cups)
Salt & pepper to taste
1 teaspoon sesame oil
2 tablespoons oyster sauce
2 teaspoons soy sauce

THICKENING BASE:

1-1/2 tablespoons cornstarch
3 tablespoons water

Fresh cilantro for garnish

Heat oil in wok on medium-high heat. Stir-fry noodles until they are browned and semi-crispy. Remove noodles from oil and set on a platter. Add more oil to wok and cook pork for 5 to 7 minutes. Add vegetables, and stir fry for 1 minute. Add remaining seasonings. Bring liquid to a boil. Add cornstarch mixture and while stirring, thicken to your preference. Add a little bit of oil to gravy just before serving...this gives it a nice shiny finish.

Raiatea Helms' Kahuku Style Garlic Shrimp

We were very lucky to have Raiatea with us because of her schedule. I've been a huge fan of Raiatea since she began singing as a teenager. Through the years she would come on my radio show and we became friends simply by supporting each other through the business. She is a very talented Hawaiian singer and she can cook! Her parents own a taro leaf company, so she decided to teach us her version of the family's Chicken Lū'au Stew and one of her favorites, Garlic Shrimp.

– Lanai Tabura

1/4 teaspoon cayenne pepper
2 tablespoons paprika
1 cup flour
1 stick butter, clarified
10 cloves garlic, finely minced
1 pound large shell-on shrimp
Salt to taste
Splash of white wine (optional)
Lemon (optional)

Mix cayenne, paprika and flour in a bowl. Cook butter until all impurities have cooked off and butter is clear. Add garlic and cook until tender (1 to 2 minutes). Coat shrimp in flour mixture and cook in garlic butter. Cook for 3 minutes on each side...salt to taste, splash of wine optional. Serve with melted butter and lemon on the side (optional).

Raiatea Helms' Chicken Lū'au Stew

6 pieces boneless/skinless chicken thighs
1 teaspoon oil
3 bay leaves
1 large piece ginger, peeled and smashed
2 cloves garlic, minced
1 quart cooked lū'au leaves
2 cans chicken broth
1 teaspoon garlic salt
1/4 teaspoon pepper
1 tablespoon cornstarch

Cut chicken into bite-sized pieces. Cook chicken in large pot with heated oil on medium-high heat. Add bay leaves, ginger and garlic. Once chicken is cooked/browned, remove bay leaves. Add cooked lū'au leaves, chicken broth and season. Mix cornstarch in a small dish with a tablespoon or two of water. Add cornstarch mixture to stew to thicken.

Mom Tabura's Spaghettini Crab Salad

Brothers Lanai & Chef Adam Tabura shared this recipe that their Mom often made while growing up on the island of Lāna'i.

– Frank Abraham

16 ounces spaghettini (thin spaghetti)
3 hard-boiled eggs, chopped
1 carrot, grated
2 tablespoons finely chopped white onion
1/4 cup sliced green onions
1/4 cup finely chopped fresh Italian parsley
1-1/2 to 2 cups mayonnaise
2 tablespoons mustard
6 ounces lump crabmeat
Salt & pepper to taste

Cook spaghettini according to package directions, drain and set aside in refrigerator to cool. Place eggs and carrots in large bowl with onions, green onions and parsley. Add cooled pasta and mix well. Add mayonnaise, mustard, crabmeat and salt and pepper to taste. Refrigerate for 2 hours or more. Taste and adjust seasoning and mayonnaise before serving. Serves 8.

CHRIS SOUZA'S OKAZUYA-STYLE CHOW FUN

Chris Souza is a dear friend of the family and is like a sister to my Mom. She was very supportive when I first created the website and contributed a lot of her personal recipes and recipes collected from the many friends that she made while working at Curves in Mānoa, which she owned for many years. This recipe is an example of the local-style of cooking that she shares.

– Frank Abraham

1 tablespoon oil
1/2 pound char siu or pork, sliced thin
1/2 pound luncheon meat or ham, sliced thin
1 (almond-size) piece ginger, mashed
1/2 cup thinly sliced carrots
1/2 cup thinly sliced celery
1/2 small onion, thinly sliced
12-ounce package bean sprouts
2 teaspoons salt
1 tablespoon oyster sauce
1 tablespoon Aloha Shoyu (soy sauce)
1/4 teaspoon MSG (optional)
1 (7-ounce) package chow fun noodles, cooked
2 stalks green onion, cut 1-inch

Heat oil on medium-high heat in skillet or wok. Add char siu, luncheon meat, and ginger. Cook until lightly browned. Add carrots, celery, and onions and cook until half done. Add bean sprouts, salt, oyster sauce, shoyu and MSG; stir lightly. Add chow fun and green onions. Cook for 1 minute.

FRANK ABRAHAM'S
CRISPY GAU GEE (WONTONS)

1 to 2 pounds cooked medium/large shrimp (if tails are still on, be sure to remove tails)
2 pounds ground pork
2 to 3 eggs
1 bunch green onions, chopped
2 cans water chestnuts, chopped
1 to 2 packets dashi seasoning or saimin packets
4 tablespoons sesame oil
2 to 3 tablespoons Aloha Shoyu (soy sauce)
4 to 6 tablespoons oyster sauce
1 tablespoon salt
Pepper
Oil for deep frying
250 to 300 wonton skins/wrappers

In a food processor, put shrimp and pulse until you have a fine paste. You may have to do it in batches. Put ground shrimp into a large mixing bowl. Put ground pork in food processor with 1 egg at a time and ground it into a paste. Do this in 2 to 3 batches. Pour the pork/egg mixture into the large mixing bowl. Mix pork and shrimp until well combined. Add remaining ingredients and mix well.

Note: Sometimes its difficult to get the proper seasoning. You might want to test the mixture by taking a teaspoonful and cooking it in a small frying pan and taste the filling before making the gau gee. You can also cook a few samples and adjust seasoning accordingly.

Once the filling is mixed, you can heat the oil to about 350°F. You can usually tell the oil is hot enough by dropping a piece of wonton skin in the oil. If it bubbles up quickly and rises to the top, the oil

(continued on the next page)

should be hot enough. We usually make the wontons and cook them at the same time. This way the wontons don't get soggy and fall apart before cooking. Start making the gau gee by wetting the outer edges of the wrapper with water, put a good amount, about one teaspoon...then gently fold the edges to form the gau gee. You can make a rectangle or triangle shape. Fry until golden brown. Season with salt as soon as you pull gau gee out of the hot oil. Serve with sweet and sour sauce or Chinese hot mustard and shoyu.

SUGOI'S HAWAI'I GARLIC FURIKAKE CHICKEN

Sugoi's Hawai'i has become a local staple for signature local plate lunches including their Garlic Furikake Chicken and Teri Loco Moco. The restaurant was featured on "The Secret Life Of" segment on the Food Network! When the segment aired, I immediately wrote Zack Lee, one of the owners, asking for the recipe and he graciously wrote back and shared two recipes with me. Be sure to visit their website: www.sugoihawaii.com.

– Frank Abraham

6 boneless chicken thighs
Salt
Mochiko flour
Sugoi's Garlic Sauce*
Oil for deep frying
Furikake

Salt chicken, roll in mochiko flour, deep fry in hot oil for 11 minutes or until golden brown and crispy. Pull chicken from hot oil and immediately dip into Sugoi Garlic Sauce. Sprinkle with furikake and serve immediately with rice and macaroni salad!

*You can substitute Sugoi's Garlic Sauce with a basic teriyaki sauce.

Sugoi's Hawai'i Teri Loco Moco

16 ounces ground beef
2 ounces ground pork
1 egg
1 onion, diced
Garlic salt
Freshly ground black pepper
Worcestershire sauce
1-1/2 cups panko (Japanese bread crumbs)
1 cup cooked rice
4 eggs, cooked, poached or fried
Teriyaki sauce
Frank Abraham's Killer Brown Gravy (page 32)

Mix the first 8 ingredients (beef through panko) together and form into 4 patties. Grill or broil patties to desired doneness, about 5 minutes on each side. Divide rice between 4 plates and top each with a patty, 1 egg, teriyaki sauce, and gravy.

DEIRDRE TODD'S HANAMĀ'ULU-STYLE SHRIMP

When I first created the recipe website CookingHawaiianStyle.com, I needed a lot of recipes. What good is a recipe website without a lot of recipes? I put out an ad and to my amazement, Deirdre replied to my ad. I couldn't have asked for a better person than Deirdre to help me fill the site with recipes. She has her own cookbooks (*Deirdre's Table Talk*) and is a food industry veteran having cooked in some of Hawai'i's top restaurants with many of Hawai'i's top chefs, and worked as a caterer. You will see a lot of Deirdre's recipes throughout the website and I honestly would not have been able to do this without her expertise and help. I need to get her on the show! Be sure to visit her website: www.ddstabletalk.com

– Frank Abraham

2 pounds shrimp, peeled, deveined
4 tablespoons brown sugar
3 tablespoons Aloha Shoyu (soy sauce)
3 tablespoons oyster sauce
2 teaspoons ground ginger
1 teaspoon sesame seed oil
1-inch piece of ginger, peeled, grated
Oil for frying
1 cup cornstarch, as needed

In a ziplock bag, combine all ingredients except oil and cornstarch. Marinate shrimp for 3 hours or overnight, if possible. In a large skillet or fryer, heat at least 1 to 2 inches of oil to 350°F. Dredge shrimp in cornstarch and deep fry until golden brown and cooked through. Serves 4 to 6.

Deirdre Todd's
Mai Tai Soo (Chop Suey Cake)

3 cups shredded turnip
3 cups iced water
2 teaspoons salt
1-1/2 cups minced Chinese roast pork
1/2 cup dried shrimp, soaked in sherry, drained, minced
1/2 cup chopped green onion
1/2 cup coarsely chopped water chestnuts
5 dried shiitake mushrooms, soaked, drained, minced
1/2 teaspoon sugar
1/2 teaspoon white pepper
2 (8-ounce) refrigerator buttermilk golden flake rolls
1 large egg, beaten
Sesame seeds

WASABI SHOYU DIPPING SAUCE:

1 tablespoon wasabi paste
Dash of Sriracha (chili hot sauce)
2 tablespoons Aloha Shoyu (soy sauce)
2 tablespoons rice wine vinegar

In a mixing bowl, soak shredded turnip in water and salt for 1 hour. Drain well; squeeze out excess water. Preheat oven to 375°F. Lightly grease a baking sheet. In a mixing bowl, combine pork, shrimp, green onion, water chestnuts, mushrooms, sugar and pepper. On floured work surface, roll each piece of dough into a 4-inch circle. Place 1/4 cup of turnip mixture into center of roll. Pinch bottom to seal. Place seam side down on prepared sheet. Brush with egg and sprinkle with sesame seeds. Bake 10 to 15 minutes until lightly browned. Serve with wasabi shoyu dipping sauce. Makes 20.

WASABI SHOYU DIPPING SAUCE:

In a mixing bowl, combine ingredients. Set aside until ready to serve.

FRANK ABRAHAM'S KILLER BROWN GRAVY

I know I'm not the only one that has tried to make the popular brown gravy that smothers our hamburger steak plate lunches and makes it so 'ono. This recipe is surprisingly easy and quick to make and it beats any of the bottled, packet or canned gravies in the market. The gravy is so rich and tasty, I guarantee you will be licking your plate!

- Frank Abraham

2 tablespoons butter
1/4 cup flour (Wondra flour works best)
1 beef bouillon cube
1 can beef broth
Salt & pepper to taste
Splash Aloha Shoyu (soy sauce)
Splash cream or milk

In frying pan of drippings from hamburger patties, melt butter over medium-high heat. Once butter has melted, add flour and cook for a few minutes stirring with a whisk to prevent burning until the flour turns a nice light brown color. This adds a richer flavor to the gravy. Add bouillon cube to mixture in frying pan and smash it down into the mixture. Add beef broth and stir quickly as the gravy thickens and forms. Keep stirring gravy using a whisk.

Add salt, pepper to taste, a splash of shoyu, and a splash of milk or cream to give the gravy a nice rich flavor. Some people have been known to add a splash of ketchup to give it that reddish brown color and extra layer of flavor.

Note: This recipe assumes that you are making hamburger steak and have leftover drippings in the pan. If you don't have drippings, I would double the amount of butter so that you have enough fat.

Frank Abraham's Hamburger Curry

1/2 block butter
1/2 onion, finely chopped
4 stalks celery, finely chopped
1 pound ground beef
1 potato cooked, peeled and cubed (optional)
1 tablespoon salt
2 to 3 tablespoons curry powder (to taste)
1 (5-ounce) can evaporated milk
1 package frozen mixed vegetables
1/4 cup Aloha Shoyu (soy sauce)

THICKENER:

1/4 cup flour
1/2 cup water

Melt butter in pot or saucepan, add onions and celery and cook until onions are opaque. Add ground beef and cook for 10 minutes or until browned. Cook potato in microwave for 4 minutes, peel, cube and set aside. Add salt and curry powder to ground beef mixture and allow to cook for 5 minutes. Add milk, mixed vegetables, potato and shoyu and simmer for 10 minutes. If you desire more sauce, add milk.

THICKEN CURRY:

Mix flour and water in a bowl stirring quickly to prevent lumps. Add more water if necessary to create a smooth, thick paste. Add mixture one mixing spoon at a time and stir rapidly into curry. Add enough mixture to reach desired thickness.

Frank Abraham's Chinese Roast Style Fried Chicken

3 pounds chicken
   drumettes or thighs
1/2 cup buttermilk
4 packages Noh Chinese
   Roast Chicken
   Seasoning Packets
4 eggs, scrambled in bowl
1/2 cup milk
4 cups all purpose flour
4 tablespoons Noh
   Chinese Roast Chicken
   Seasoning
Oil for frying

Mix chicken, buttermilk and 3 packets of Noh Chinese Roast Chicken seasoning. Mix well and allow to marinate overnight if possible. When ready to cook, heat oil. Scramble 4 eggs in a bowl and add 1/2 cup of milk. Set aside. Sift flour with 1 packet of Noh Chinese roast chicken seasoning. Dredge chicken pieces in flour, then egg, then flour again. Allow dredged pieces to sit for 15 minutes before frying. Heat oil in a deep pot to 350 to 360°F. Fry chicken pieces for about 15 to 20 minutes or until juices run clear.

Senator Daniel Inouye's Sweet & Sour Spare Ribs

I contacted Senator Inouye's office requesting a recipe for the website and they graciously wrote back with a letter in the mail and this recipe attached. An excerpt from the letter read, "This recipe was given to me by former state senator John Ushijima in 1950 when we were both in Law school at George Washington University in Washington, D.C."
- Frank Abraham

3 pounds pork spare ribs
1/3 cup flour
1/3 cup shoyu (soy sauce)
3/4 cup vinegar
1 cup water
1/2 cup brown sugar, packed
1 teaspoon salt
1 clove garlic
1-inch ginger root
Dash of five spices (Chinese five spice)

Cut spare ribs into 2 x 2-inch pieces. Marinate in flour and soy sauce for 30 minutes. Brown in cooking oil. Add the rest of ingredients and simmer for 45 minutes or until tender. May be served with chunks of fresh or canned pineapple.

CHEF IPPY AIONA'S PORK BELLY ADOBO

Chef Ippy grew up in his parent's kitchen on Hawai'i Island and has a great spirit about him. He was introduced to the world on *Next Food Network Star*. I met the chef doing a comedy show in one of his restaurants, 3 Fat Pigs. He loves working with pork and is very good doing it. Whenever you visit Hawai'i Island, make sure you check out 3 Fat Pigs and his plate lunch restaurant Ippy's Hawaiian BBQ. When Ippy stopped by the *Cooking Hawaiian Style* show he made an amazing pork belly adobo! Make this one for your friends and 'ohana and watch them say, "Wow."

– Lanai Tabura

MARINADE:

1 orange, sliced
1 lemon, sliced
2 cups apple cider vinegar
    or sugar cane vinegar
2 garlic cloves, crushed
2 bay leaves, crushed
1 cup water

2 pounds pork belly
3 to 4 tablespoons cooking oil
2 cloves garlic, crushed
6 to 8 peppercorns
2 bay leaves, crushed
1 tablespoon Dijon mustard
1/2 cup Aloha Shoyu (soy sauce)
2 cans coconut milk
2 cups brown sugar

Put marinade ingredients in a large glass bowl or Ziplock bag. Place pork belly in marinade and soak overnight, if possible.

Take pork out of marinade and slice into 2-inch cubes. Reserve marinade.

Brown pork on medium-high heat in oil with garlic, peppercorns, bay leaves and Dijon mustard. Once browned, add enough of the marinade used earlier to barely cover meat. Add shoyu, coconut milk and sugar. Cook on medium/low heat until tender about 1 to 2 hours.

Chef Ippy Aiona's Beef Steak Tataki

1 New York steak

MARINADE:

2 cups red wine
2 tablespoons sugar
1 sprig fresh thyme
1/2 onion, chopped

PICKLED ONIONS:

3 cups red wine vinegar
1 cup water
1 cup sugar
1 red onion, sliced thin

AIOLI:

1/2 cup mayonnaise
1/2 cup grainy mustard

Marinade steak in red wine, sugar, fresh thyme and an onion cut in half. Marinate overnight if possible, or for at least 1 to 2 hours. Remove steak from marinade, grill on each side for 2 minutes, remove from grill and cut against the grain into thin slices.

PICKLED ONIONS:

Bring vinegar, water, and sugar to boil in a sauté pan. Add onion. Cook for 5 to 10 minutes on medium-high heat until onions are tender. This is a short-cut pickling method.

AIOLI:

Mix equal parts of mayonnaise and grainy mustard in a small dish or bowl.

Spread mustard aioli on the bottom of a serving platter, put pieces of steak over the mustard and top with pickled onions.

CHAPTER 3

BACK TO OUR ROOTS

Daniel Anthony's Instant Pa'i 'Ai Kulolo

I met Daniel Anthony about 12 years ago at the Island 98.5 radio station. I have this soft spot in my heart for local people who hustle to put food on the table. I try to help however I can. Daniel always has this vibe about him that is happy and filled with Aloha. He came on the show because he was selling lychee by the pound in Wai'anae, and I thought, "Here is a local boy making an honest living. Let's promote him." We have been friends ever since and I've always had the utmost respect for him. Today, he has been sharing with the world the power of taro, how it brings people together, and the value it has to all of us. He has this gift of speaking to the community through what he loves doing. The best part of Daniel is he is a family man who enjoys sharing. Here he shares 2 of his favorite recipes: Instant Pa'i 'ai Kulolo and Koena Meatloaf.

– Lanai Tabura

1 cup coconut milk
1/2 cup raw sugar
4 cups pa'i 'ai, grated with cheese grater

Reduce coconut milk and sugar in a pan, gradually add grated pa'i 'ai and mix until creamy. Serve hot or chill. Top with fresh fruit, whipped cream, or whatever makes you happy!

Daniel Anthony's Koena Meatloaf

2 pounds Kualoa organic ground beef (or your favorite brand)
1-1/2 pounds koena (clean taro scrapings or use grated pa'i 'ai)
3 eggs
1 tablespoon Hawaiian salt
1 ounce Worcestershire Sauce
1 teaspoon black pepper
Up to 4 cups of vegetables cut into 1/2-inch cubes (carrots, onions, celery,
    bell peppers)

Preheat oven to 400°F. Add all ingredients in large mixing bowl, mix
thoroughly. Put into ceramic baking pan. Cook for 35 to 45 minutes.

KALEO PILANCA'S HAMBURGER WATERCRESS WITH CHOMORRO RIBS & FINADENE SAUCE

Kaleo has been a very good friend of mine for over 10 years now. We worked together doing morning radio and traveled a lot doing stand up comedy all over the mainland. This guy can make you laugh and make you feel good with his cooking. Kaleo and I were lucky enough to cook for Anthony Bourdain for his TV show on the Travel Channel, and it's a day we will never forget and always talk about. We kept it real that day, cooking stuffed Onaga, and Kaleo's stew lū'au. Anthony loved it! Kaleo and I try to get together often to barbecue and he is famous for cooking his saboas or soup. I always thought he should bottle his Chomorro Finadene Sauce, but now he shares it with you in this book.

– Lanai Tabura

HAMBURGER WATERCRESS:

3 cloves garlic
1 pound ground beef
1 to 2 bunches watercress
1 cup Aloha Shoyu (soy sauce)
2 cups chicken broth
Salt & pepper to taste

CHOMORRO RIBS:

Garlic, chopped
White onion, chopped
Green onion, chopped
Lemon, juiced
1 cup white vinegar
1 cup Aloha Shoyu (soy sauce)
2 to 3 pounds pork ribs

FINADENE SAUCE:

4 to 6 cloves garlic, chopped
3 to 7 Hawaiian chili peppers, chopped
1 bunch green onion, chopped
1 lemon, juiced
1 cup white vinegar
1 cup shoyu (soy sauce)

HAMBURGER WATERCRESS:

Add oil to pan, mince garlic and add to hot oil. Add ground beef and brown. Remove excess fat. Cut watercress into bite-sized pieces and add to pot. Stir ingredients in pot adding soy sauce and chicken broth. I usually like to add enough broth to cover the ground beef and watercress and add the shoyu to taste starting with 1/4 cup and adding more as necessary. Add salt and pepper. Simmer and serve over hot rice!

CHOMORRO RIBS:

Mix all ingredients except ribs in large pot and let sit for at least 20 minutes. Cook ribs on grill until 3/4 done (about 60 minutes). Put pot with sauce on stovetop and bring to boil on high heat. Add ribs to boiling sauce and reduce heat to medium. Cook for an additional 20 minutes.

FINADENE SAUCE:

Mix ingredients and serve over grilled ribs. It also tastes great over steak, chicken, or your favorite food.

Colleen Hanabusa's Fresh 'Ahi Pasta

The first time I met Colleen Hanabusa was at a fundraiser, and I immediately loved her. She is not just a politician but a great human being and local girl from Hawai'i. Her demeanor is Aloha and she is very passionate about what she does. I am friends with some of her staff and they always rave about her culinary skills which she flexes for them in Washington, D.C. When she is not on the Hill, you can find her cooking for her homesick staff from Hawai'i. I really like her 'Ahi Pasta, and I am sure you will, too! Here is Congress Woman Colleen Hanabusa's Fresh 'Ahi Pasta and Clam Pasta.

— Lanai Tabura

1 pound linguine pasta
2 tablespoons olive oil
Salt & pepper to taste
1/2 pound 'ahi (more if you want), cut into cubes
1 to 1-1/2 tablespoons country Dijon mustard
Juice of 1/2 lemon
2 cloves garlic, minced
2-inch piece of ginger, slivered
1/2 sweet Maui onion, sliced
Parsley, chopped, to taste
Basil, chopped, to taste
Oregano, chopped, to taste
4 large shiitake mushroom caps, sliced
2 tablespoons vermouth or sake
6 large black olives, sliced
1 teaspoon capers
Red shoga ginger (sushi kind), sliced
Shredded nori for garnish
Sesame seeds for garnish

Cook pasta al dente because you will finish cooking in the pan. Heat frying pan on medium-high heat and add half of the olive oil. Salt and pepper the 'ahi cubes and sear in the oil. Remove and add mustard, lemon juice, half of the garlic and ginger. Remove from pan and set aside. Add remaining olive oil to pan and sauté the sliced onion. As it cooks, add the remaining garlic and ginger. Also season with basil and oregano. Add the mushrooms when onions are done, and deglaze pan with vermouth or sake.

Add the 'ahi back into the pan and cook until 'ahi is heated through. Add olives, and pasta. Toss together and add capers and parsley. If needed, add a little olive oil. Finish with an additional squeeze of lemon juice and remainder of Dijon mustard. Garnish with shoga ginger, nori, and sesame seeds.

Colleen Hanabusa's Clam Pasta

1 tablespoon olive oil
1/2 onion, sliced
Salt & pepper to taste
2 to 3 basil leaves, chopped
1 teaspoon oregano
Fresh or canned mushrooms (easier if sliced)
1 can chopped clams (separate clams from juice)
2 tablespoons vermouth
1/4 cup black olives, sliced
1 sprig fresh parsley, chopped
1/2 pound linguine, cooked
1 tablespoon butter
Parmesan cheese (optional)

Heat pan with oil on medium-high heat. Sauté the onions for 1 to 2 minutes until translucent. Add salt, pepper, basil and oregano. Add mushrooms and clams. Deglaze the pan with vermouth. Add olives and put the clam juice and parsley. Adjust salt and pepper if necessary and add butter and a little olive oil for richness. Serve over pasta with parsley on top and add Parmesan cheese if you wish.

MELVEEN LEED'S CRUSTACEAN POLYNESIA

Melveen Leed, the tita from Moloka'i, is a household name in Hawai'i's music world. Melveen won best female artist at the Nā Hōkū Hanohano awards not 1 but 5 times. Not only can she sing, she has a great sense of humor and can cook! We were happy to have Melveen on *Cooking Hawaiian Style* a few times. She lived in Tahiti for a while and shared a great Tahitian-influenced dish, Crustacean Polynesia.

– Lanai Tabura

4 to 5 cups fresh or canned coconut milk
1 tomato
1 Maui onion, diced small
4 to 5 pounds of your favorite seafood: whole crab, cut up; lobster tail, cut in half; clams; shrimp (shell on)
Salt & pepper to taste

In a large pot, put coconut milk, tomato, onion and stir. Then immediately add crustaceans and stir all ingredients together. Cover pot and cook on medium-high heat until it starts to boil, then reduce to simmer. Dish is ready when you see the crab, shrimp and lobster turn red. Salt and pepper to taste.

Popo June Tong's Pork Hash

June Tong, or "Popo" as she is known, has 2 cookbooks out but has an arsenal of great Chinese-Hawai'i-style recipes. This lady is an amazing chef and a great, kind person. I had the chance to have dinner with her and some of her closest friends up in Palolo Valley. She made us a feast that night and we got to talk story about food and cooking. You can tell she has a deep passion for what she does and really enjoys being in the kitchen. One of my new favorite pūpū is her Shrimp Toast.

– Lanai Tabura

1 pound ground pork
1 teaspoon cornstarch
1 tablespoon shoyu (soy sauce)
1 tablespoon sesame oil
Salt to taste

Combine ingredients and mix well in a bowl. Place bowl in steamer and cook for 35 minutes. Garnish and serve.

Popo June Tong's Shrimp Toast

SHRIMP FILLING:

1 pound shrimp, peeled and deveined
1/4 pound bacon, minced
1/4 pound ground pork
1/4 cup water chestnuts, minced
1/4 cup cilantro, minced
1 egg white
2 tablespoons cornstarch
Salt & pepper to taste
2 cups oil for frying

TOAST:

4 slices white bread, crust trimmed, cut into triangles

Combine shrimp filling ingredients and mix well. Refrigerate for 2 hours. Take pieces of bread and place enough filling on bread and mound firmly onto each slice. Heat oil to 350°F and fry shrimp toast facing down for 1 minute. Turn and cook until golden brown. Drain on paper towels.

LANAI TABURA'S MOM'S PINAKBET

1/2 pound pork longanisa sausage
2 cloves garlic
1/2 cup water
1 thumb-size ginger
3 eggplant, sliced
1/3 cup tomatoes
1 cup pumpkin, diced
1 handful string beans
1 to 2 bittermelon, sliced (optional)
1 cup okra
Salt
2 tablespoons patis

If possible, remove skin from sausage, mince sausage. In a pot, heat one teaspoon of oil. Cook garlic and sausage for 1 to 2 minutes. Add water and bring to boil. Add all vegetables to the pot, turn heat to low and allow to cook covered for 15 minutes. Add salt, patis to taste.

DEIRDRE TODD'S CHAR SIU GIN DOI

1 pound mochiko flour
    (glutinous rice flour)
3/4 cup sugar
2-1/2 teaspoons baking powder
1-1/4 cups water
1 teaspoon gin
1/2 cup minced char sui
1/4 cup minced dried shrimp
1/4 cup minced green onion
2 tablespoons hoisin sauce
1/2 teaspoon salt
1/4 teaspoon sesame oil
1/4 teaspoon ground
    white pepper
1 cup white sesame seeds
Oil for frying

In a mixing bowl, combine mochiko, sugar, and baking powder. Stir in water and gin. Turn the dough out onto a work surface and knead until smooth, about 5 minutes. In a separate bowl, combine char sui, shrimp, green onion, hoisin sauce, salt, sesame oil and pepper. On work surface, divide dough into 20 to 24 balls. Flatten each piece with your fingers. Place a heaping tablespoon of filling in center of each piece. Pinch the edges together to seal in filling and roll into a ball. Spread sesame seeds onto a shallow dish. Roll dough balls in seeds, pressing lightly to help the seeds adhere to the dough.

In a large skillet or fryer, heat oil to 375°F. Fry dough balls, turning frequently until golden brown (6 to 7 minutes). Drain on paper towels. Makes approximately 20 to 24 doughnuts.

OOKING

HAWAIIAN

STYLE

CHAPTER 4

WITH A TWIST!

KIMI WERNER'S SMOKED 'AHI PIZZA

Kimi Werner is such an amazing human being and we were happy to have her join our show. She is most famous for her free diving talents, but is also an amazing painter and chef. Originally from Maui, now living on O'ahu, diving is still a huge part of her life as she won the National Spearfishing Championship in 2008. When you get a chance, check out Kimi's artwork at kimiwernerart.com. When she came by our kitchen, she made this amazing Smoked 'Ahi Pizza from scratch and even caught the 'ahi herself.

– Lanai Tabura

BÉCHAMEL SAUCE:

3 tablespoons butter
3 tablespoons flour
1-1/2 cups whole milk
1/4 cup grated Parmesan cheese
Dash nutmeg
Garlic salt
Dash white pepper

CRUST:

1 to 2 tablespoons butter
2 cloves garlic, minced
Chia flat bread (from the Costco bakery)

MIXTURE/TOPPING:

1 (6-ounce) container Hāmākua
    mushrooms
1 Maui onion, thinly sliced
1 pound smoked 'ahi
Handful arugula or spinach
1 cup grated Havarti cheese

GARNISH:

Truffle oil
Balsamic reduction (optional)

BÉCHAMEL SAUCE:

Melt butter in small saucepan, add flour and cook the flour in the butter for 1 to 2 minutes. Slowly whisk in milk until smooth and creamy and until you achieve the consistency of an alfredo sauce. Add cheese, nutmeg, garlic salt and pepper to taste. Set aside.

continued on page 58

CRUST:

In a pan, sauté butter and garlic and grill slices of chia flat bread until golden brown. Set flat bread aside.

MIXTURE/TOPPING:

Add the mushrooms, onions, and 'ahi to the same pan used with the butter and garlic and sauté ingredients just enough to cook the mushrooms. Put grilled chia flat bread onto cookie sheet, spread with béchamel sauce, then mushroom-'ahi mixture. Top with 3 to 4 leaves of arugula and grated cheese. Bake at 450°F for 6 to 7 minutes, remove when cheese is nice and melted. Drizzle with white truffle oil or a balsamic reduction.

ONDA PASTA'S KAHUKU SHRIMP & FRESH PASTA

Onda Pasta brings us Italy and Hawai'i blended together from the North Shore. We asked these guys to come on the show to share some of their great no-preservatives pastas. Owned by Andrea and Jessica Onetti you can find them at events all around the island serving up their dishes. Andrea is a classically trained chef from Rome, Italy and knows his stuff. We had a great time in the kitchen as he made us some Onda Pasta and Kahuku Shrimp!

– Lanai Tabura

2 tablespoons olive oil
1 tablespoon butter
1 clove garlic, minced
2 handfuls cherry tomatoes, cut in half
12 Kahuku (or fresh) shrimp, cleaned and deveined
1 to 2 teaspoons flour (optional)
1 lemon wedge
1/2 cup white wine
Salt, pepper and chili flakes to taste
Parsley, minced
1/2 pound of fresh pasta
Parmesan cheese

Start boiling a pot of water for your pasta, then begin making your sauce.

In a large pan big enough to hold the sauce and pasta, warm the oil and butter together in a pan on medium heat. Add the garlic and sauté until golden. Add the tomatoes and sauté for 1 to 2 minutes then add the shrimp. Sauté until the shrimp starts turning pink, then sprinkle 1 teaspoon of flour and stir until the flour mixes in with all of the liquid. Squeeze 5 to 10 drops of lemon juice, then add the wine, salt, pepper and chili flakes to taste and a pinch of parsley. Allow the sauce to cook until the alcohol has evaporated and the sauce is nice and thick. Remove from heat. Taste sauce and adjust seasoning if necessary.

Toss pasta in the boiling water and cook until al dente, or until it is still slightly firm. Strain pasta, reserving 1 ladle of the cooking water. If the consistency of the sauce is too thick, you may add a few table-spoons of the cooking water to the pan. Add the pasta to the pan of sauce and return to high heat. Flip the pasta around in the pan until the sauce gets a nice creamy consistency and the pasta is coated and cooked uniformly.

Place the pasta on two plates, dividing the shrimp and tomatoes equally. Sprinkle each with a small amount of Parmesan and pars-ley and serve immediately.

OLENA HEU'S BOMBUCHA SALAD WITH SEARED POKE & LILIKO'I VINAIGRETTE

Olena and I have been friends for a long time, meeting at the radio station. I just started Island 98.5 and she was doing promotions with our sister station. She has this great smile and outgoing personality that everyone loves. She is from Kaua'i and I think we have that country connection going on. You can find her on KHON2 Wake Up Today every morning giving you the news and having some fun. I got to work with her there for another 9 months or so doing Lanai's App of the Day and it was a blast. Olena is very talented not only in front of the TV camera but is also known for holding the Miss Hawai'i title in 2004. On the show she taught me how to make one of her comfort foods, Seared Poke with a Liliko'i Dressing.

– Lanai Tabura

SEARED POKE:

1 package Noh Poke Seasoning
1/2 pound 'ahi, cubed
1 tablespoon sesame oil

SALAD:

1 head romaine lettuce
1 tomato, sliced
1 cucumber, sliced
1/2 package fresh mushrooms, sliced
1 red and yellow bell pepper, slivered
4 sprigs of Cilantro
1 stalk celery, sliced
Goat cheese chèvre
Wonton chips (optional)
Cashews or macadamia nuts (optional)

LILIKO'I VINAIGRETTE:

1/2 cup Aunty Liliko'i unsweetened
    passion fruit juice
1 cup rice wine vinegar
1 cup extra virgin olive oil
2 tablespoons Hawaiian honey
Pinch salt
Pepper
1 Hawaiian chili pepper

SEARED POKE

Prepare poke mix by soaking ogo in water as instructed. Cut 'ahi into 1-inch cubes, mix ingredients, heat skillet and flash fry poke in sesame oil for 1 to 2 minutes.

SALAD

Cut all vegetables for salad and place in bowl. Add seared poke to top of salad and garnish as you prefer with nuts, wonton chips, cheese, etc.

VINAIGRETTE

Add all ingredients to blender and blend well. Chill until ready to use.

RAYMOND NOH'S POKE TRIO

I met Raymond at the KGMB 9 studios about 13 years ago when I was hired to do one of his Noh Brand commercials. Raymond is the CEO of Noh Foods, a family business that has been around for over 50 years making spices in a packet for local people to make there favorite dishes. His dad was a genius in the kitchen, coming up with ways to just add water to all the ingredients to make Kim Chee, Kalbi Sauce, and Adobo, to name a few. Raymond is one of the best storytellers I know and the guy has a heart of gold. I am happy to call him one of my good friends, and today he shares with us some of his family's favorites.

– Lanai Tabura

SALMON POKE:

1/2 pound salmon, cubed
1/2 cup Noh BBQ Sauce
Salt
Green onions, for garnish

TAKO POKE:

1/2 pound cooked tako (octopus), sliced thin
Noh Hawaiian Hot Sauce, to taste
Green onions, for garnish

'AHI POKE:

1 pound 'ahi, cubed
1 package Noh Poke Mix
2 tablespoons sesame oil

SALMON POKE:

Cube salmon, add Noh BBQ Sauce, salt and green onions for garnish. Mix and serve! Top with crème fraîche or sour cream, optional.

TAKO POKE:

Slice cooked tako, mix with Noh hot sauce and garnish with green onions. Add a splash of Aloha Shoyu and sesame oil if you want. Thats it!

'AHI POKE:

Cube 'ahi, soak ogo in bowl of water for 1 minute. Chop ogo, add contents of poke mix and ogo, sesame oil and mix. Serve!

Raymond Noh's Kim Chee Steak

1 ribeye or favorite steak
Pinch Hawaiian salt
Pinch fresh ground peppercorns
1 package Noh Kim Chee seasoning
Sesame or cooking oil

Heat oil in pan. Season steak with Hawaiian salt and fresh ground peppercorns. When pan is hot, put steak in pan. Sprinkle with kim chee seasoning. After 5 minutes, turn steak over and season again.

BETTY SHIMABUKURO'S RAMEN BURGER

etty has been writing columns in the paper about food for as long as I can remember. I think it was the late 90s. It was cool to talk story with her and have her on the show, because she has her pulse on the cooking and food world. She has written or edited 10 cookbooks and when she joined us, she made a tapioca pudding, which is one of my favorites, and the famous Ramen Burger. I have a ton of respect for Betty because she can write and she is great at it. If you get a chance, pick up one of her cookbooks.

- Lanai Tabura

RAMEN BURGER BUNS:

1 package dry ramen noodles
(any flavor), with seasoning packets
1 egg
3 round plastic containers,
4 inches in diameter *
1/4 cup vegetable oil for frying

*This requires several plastic containers, the size that sour cream or margarine comes in.

HISAGO BURGER:

1-1/2 tablespoons dehydrated onion
1/2 cup hot water
4 slices white bread, torn in pieces
2 pounds ground beef (80% lean)
1-1/2 tablespoons minced celery
1/4 teaspoon salt, or to taste
1/4 teaspoon pepper, or to taste
1 teaspoon vegetable oil

RAMEN BURGER BUNS:

Bring pot of water to boil. Add noodles and seasoning packet. Cook until noodles are tender but not soft, 2 to 3 minutes. Drain; let cool to room temperature. Place cooked ramen noodles in bowl. Beat egg and pour over noodles, tossing to coat well. Divide noodles between 2 plastic containers. Top each with piece of plastic wrap or baking parchment. Place 1 container on top of the other. Place third container on top of stack. Place a weight such as a can of beans into the top container. Place entire stack in refrigerator and chill about 1 hour.

Heat 2 tablespoons of oil in skillet over medium-high heat. Carefully remove ramen burger buns from containers and place in oil. Fry until light brown and crisp. Add more oil to pan if necessary and turn buns. Fry until done on other side. Remove and drain on paper towels. Serves 1.

HISAGO DELICATESSEN BURGER:

Soak dehydrated onion in hot water until soft. Pour mixture over bread pieces and toss until bread falls apart and forms a soft paste (add more water if needed). Add beef, celery, salt and pepper; toss lightly to combine. Form into 8 patties about 1 inch thick. Make a depression in the center (this helps the burger cook evenly). Heat oil in skillet. Fry burgers on medium-high heat until cooked through, about 5 minutes per side.

For sandwiches use: boneless teriyaki chicken, kālua pork, teri hamburger patty (cooked), 1 piece bulgogi, sliced.

For garnish: grilled onions, arugula, chopped green onion, teriyaki or bbq sauce, chopped kim chee or any of your favorites!

Glen Shinsato's
Cured Pork Patty Sandwich

Shinsato = Sustainability. The guys at Shinsato Farm are really bringing back how we grew up in the country. The Shinsato 'ohana is teaching people that we can be independent and support ourselves in a healthy way. Shinsato Farm raises and butchers their own livestock. It was great to have them in our kitchen to share with us their clean-tasting pieces of pork. They really are educating the community about how raising our food should be—the old-fashioned way and not processed. I am a huge fan of pork chops and now their Cured Pork Patty. If you ever get a chance to visit Shinsato Farm, tell them we sent you!

1 pound ground pork
1-1/2 teaspoons Morton Tender Quick
1 tablespoon sugar
1 clove garlic, finely minced
Salt, to taste
1 egg

Mix ground pork with seasoning & salt, form patties. Fry patties in pan on medium-high heat for 10 minutes. Remove patties from frying pan and fry an egg(s) in the same pan, preferably sunny side up. While egg is frying, assemble burger with your favorite condiments, lettuce, tomato, burger and top with an egg.

Glen Shinsato's Cured Pork Chop with Arugula Butter

BRINE:

1 to 2 pork chops
1 tablespoon Morton Tender Quick
1/2 tablespoon sugar
1/2 cup water

2 tablespoons butter
1 clove garlic, minced
Handful arugula

Brine pork chops in Morton Tender Quick, sugar, and water. Let cure in refrigerator for 1 to 2 hours. Before cooking, rinse chops under running water to remove excess salt. Brown pork chops in lightly greased skillet 8 to 10 minutes. Remove from pan and add butter, garlic. Allow garlic to cook for a few minutes, toss arugula in pan, just enough to wilt the arugula.

SID ALAPAI'S ADOBO FRIED CHICKEN

Sid popped up from no-where. When I first launched the website, Sid was one of those people who immediately jumped in and started contributing recipes. I love the contributions that Sid has made—his style of cook-ing is real local and home style.
– Frank Abraham

3 pounds chicken thighs

MARINADE:

1 cup cider vinegar
1/2 cup Aloha Shoyu (soy sauce)
2 cloves garlic, minced
1 teaspoon ground peppercorns
2 bay leaves

DREDGE:

3 eggs, lightly beaten
1/2 cup flour
1/2 cup cornstarch
1 teaspoon salt
1 teaspoon garlic salt
1 teaspoon pepper
Oil for deep frying

Soak the chicken in adobo marinade for 30 to 60 minutes. Add chicken and marinade to a pot and bring to boil, then simmer for 40 minutes. In a pot deep enough for frying, heat oil to 350°F. Remove chicken from pot and set on rack to allow ex-cess liquid to drain. Beat egg in bowl. Add dry ingredients in a dif-ferent bowl. Dredge chicken in flour, then egg, then flour again. Fry chicken in hot oil for 20 minutes or until golden brown.

Frank Abraham's Kālua Lū'au Lasagna Rolls with Haupia Béchamel Sauce

2 packages frozen taro leaves (lū'au) or you can use spinach
8 lasagna noodles, prepared according to directions
6 tablespoons butter (use margarine or oil for vegetarian)
6 tablespoons flour
2 (12-ounce) cans of coconut milk
Salt & pepper to taste
1 container kālua pork or 1 pound homemade kālua pork
1/4 cup milk

Empty lū'au leaves into a sieve and squeeze out all of the excess liquid. Set aside. Prepare lasagna noodles. Once cooked, set aside. Melt butter or margarine in sauce pan. Once butter is melted add flour slowly, whisking constantly. Cook flour for about 1 minute. Slowly add coconut milk whisking constantly to maintain a smooth consistency. Salt and pepper to taste. Set béchamel aside.

Divide lū'au leaves into 8 equal portions. Take a piece of lasagna noodle and spread the lū'au leaf across 3/4 of the length of the pasta. Take kālua pork and spread across 3/4 of the length of the pasta. Spread about 2 tablespoons of the béchamel over the taro leaves and kālua pork and roll. Carefully place rolled lasagna into a shallow 8 x 8-inch glass or ceramic baking pan. Complete until all 8 rolls are complete. Take remaining béchamel and thin it out with milk and pour over lasagna rolls. Bake covered at 325°F for 20 to 25 minutes.

Frank Abraham's Teriyaki Chicken Skewers With Fresh Tomato Chimichurri

TOMATO CHIMICHURRI:

1/4 cup minced parsley
1/4 cup minced cilantro
1 medium heirloom tomato, cut into cubes
1 garlic clove, grated
1 to 2 Hawaiian chili peppers, finely minced
1/3 cup extra virgin olive oil
Juice from 1/2 lemon + more to taste
Zest from 1 lemon
Sea salt to taste

TERIYAKI GLAZE:

1/4 cup Aloha Shoyu (soy sauce)
1/4 cup water
1/4 cup brown sugar
1 clove garlic
1 slice fresh ginger
1 tablespoon cornstarch
2 tablespoons water

1 to 2 pounds chicken, cut into pieces
24 BBQ skewers (soaked in water for 30 minutes to prevent burning)

CHIMICHURRI:

Chop parsley, cilantro, tomatoes and mix in bowl. Add garlic and Hawaiian chili peppers. Slowly drizzle olive oil, lemon juice, lemon zest and salt. Toss and set aside in refrigerator.

TERIYAKI GLAZE :

Add first five ingredients in a small pot and heat over medium heat until the brown sugar is completely dissolved. In a small bowl, add cornstarch and water and mix thoroughly until cornstarch is dissolved. Slowly add a little of the corn starch mixture a teaspoon at a time and cook for 5 minutes. Repeat until the desired thickness is achieved. Divide sauce in half. Use half for basting chicken on grill and the other half to drizzle on finished dish.

Cut chicken into 1-inch pieces and place 3 to 6 pieces on skewers that have been soaking in water for at least 30 minutes. Sprinkle with a little bit of salt and pepper and grill. Brush teriyaki glaze on chicken and cook for 3 to 4 minutes on each side. Place cooked chicken skewers on plate and drizzle with spicy tomato chimichurri and teriyaki glaze.

LANAI TABURA'S SNAPPER EGG FOO YOUNG

Ginger, slivered
Tomatoes, diced
Bean sprouts
Carrots, slivered
Bell peppers, slivered
Tofu, cubed
1 to 2 ounces 'ōpakapaka, thinly sliced
4 fresh eggs, scrambled
Green onions, sliced

SAUCE:

1 teaspoon hoisin sauce
2 tablespoons oyster sauce
1/2 teaspoon sesame oil
1 teaspoon honey

Heat pan with a little bit of oil. Sauté your favorite vegetables/ingredients in hot pan. Be sure not to overcook. Add fish and toss until cooked. Scramble eggs in a bowl. Add scrambled eggs to pan with fish and vegetables. Garnish with chopped fried onions and green onions, optional. Finish with sauce.

SAUCE:

Mix all ingredients in a bowl until honey is dissolved and all ingredients are combined well. Set aside and use as a garnish to top egg foo young.

Sai Kairod's
Cilantro Chili Chicken Skewers

Although he was born in Thailand, Sai Kairod spent most of his life in Hawai'i. Sai takes the best of Thai and Hawaiian-style cooking and shares some of his amazing recipes with us.

– Frank Abraham

2 pounds boneless/skinless chicken thighs
   or breast meat
1/4 cup extra virgin olive oil
6 cloves garlic, minced
3/4 bunch fresh cilantro
   (save remaining for garnish)
1 teaspoon salt & pepper
Sweet chili sauce for basting

Soak skewers in water for at least 20 minutes to prevent burning. Cut chicken into 1-inch cubes and place into bowl. Add olive oil, garlic, and cilantro in a food processor and pulverize. Pour the marinade into the bowl with the chicken, add teaspoon of salt and pepper and marinate overnight if possible. Preheat the grill to medium heat and coat with oil. Remove chicken from the refrigerator and put 5 to 6 pieces of chicken on each skewer. Cook for 4 to 5 minutes on each side. Brush chili sauce on chicken just before done cooking to create a nice glaze.

blah

LORI IKEDA'S GREEN ONION AND CHILI OIL PA'I 'AI BISCUITS

I came across Lori Ikeda's website a couple of years ago and just loved her passion for cooking and her quest to create her own bits of paradise in her everyday life, which is reflected in her cooking. I am proud to have her as an ongoing contributor to the site. Lori is a local girl who moved to California, something we can all relate to. We all have friends and family who, for one reason or another, have moved from Hawai'i to the mainland. Over the years, Lori and I have become long-distance friends. She is someone that I consider a part of the family. Although we haven't met, I feel a sense of connection... this is something that I think is unique to Hawai'i. No matter where we are, it is always special to run into another person who is from Hawai'i. It is this instant connection with each other and the longing to stay connected that makes Hawai'i so special. Visit her website at: www.guavarose.com

– Frank Abraham

4 ounces pa'i 'ai*
1/2 cup or more flour (wheat- or gluten-free blend) or biscuit mix (preferred)
1/4 cup or more water
1/2 cup green onions, chopped
Chili oil
Sea salt

Preheat oven to 400°F. Crumble pa'i 'ai on a floured surface. Knead in flour and water until a smooth dough forms. Add small amounts of flour and water if necessary while kneading the dough to get a final dough that is not sticky. If the pa'i 'ai is hard and crumbly, chop it up and crumble it in small pieces. Bring the water to a boil in a small pot. Add the crumbled pa'i 'ai and turn the heat down to medium low. As the pa'i 'ai softens, use a potato masher to mash it smooth. Turn off the heat and scoop it into a mixing bowl to cool down. Once it is lukewarm, knead in the flour until a smooth dough forms. Add extra flour/water as needed to get a final dough that is not sticky.

Knead in the green onions. Roll dough out 1/2-inch thick. Use 1-1/2- to 2-inch cutters to cut out biscuits and place them on a baking sheet. Drizzle the biscuit tops with chili oil and sprinkle lightly with sea salt. Bake for 12 to 16 minutes, or until cooked through. Cooking times may vary according to how much flour and water has been added to the dough.

You can order pa'i 'ai from anywhere in the world online at www.manaai.com and have it shipped to you. Pa'i 'ai will last indefinitely if kept in an airtight, cool place.

Lori Ikeda's Pa'i 'Ai Crackers

4 ounces pa'i 'ai*
1/2 cup or more flour
    (wheat- or gluten-free blend)
1/4 cup or more water
2 tablespoons oil
Sea salt

Preheat oven to 375°F. Crumble pa'i 'ai on a floured surface. Knead in flour and water until a smooth dough forms. Add small amounts of flour and water if necessary while kneading the dough to get a final dough that is not sticky. If the pa'i 'ai is hard and crumbly, chop it up and crumble it in small pieces. Bring the water to a boil in a small pot. Add the crumbled pa'i 'ai and turn the heat down to medium low. As the pa'i 'ai softens, use a potato masher to mash it smooth. Turn off the heat and scoop it into a mixing bowl to cool down. Once it is luke-warm, knead in the flour until a smooth dough forms. Add extra flour/water as needed to get a final dough that is not sticky.

Coat the bottom of a shiny baking sheet (12 x 17 inches) with the oil. Place the dough onto the sheet pan and roll out as thin as possible. Sprinkle the top lightly with sea salt. Bake for 15 minutes, then turn the whole cracker sheet over and bake another 10 minutes. It should look crispy and mostly golden brown all around the sides. The middle may still look a little light colored, but if you leave it in the oven longer, the outside edges will get too brown and taste burnt. Let the cracker sheet cool down a bit before breaking it into pieces. If desired, place the light colored middle pieces (which may still be slightly soft) back into the turned off oven to crisp them up. Check it after 5 minutes and remove it if it has crisped up. Don't leave it in too long or it will get over-browned.

*You can order pa'i 'ai from anywhere in the world online at www.manaai.com and have it shipped to you. Pa'i 'ai will last indefinitely if kept in an airtight, cool place.

Karolyn Fujimoto's Yakisoba Egg Rolls

 arolyn runs a popular food blog on www.Foodjimoto.com. I approached her when I first started the website as she had a lot of recipes with a Hawaii influence. When I saw her recipe for Yakisoba Egg Rolls, I had to write and ask her to share her recipes on my website. She has been an ongoing contributor ever since.

-Frank Abraham

1/4 onion, sliced
2 slices fresh ginger, minced
1 clove garlic, minced
4 Nappa cabbage (leaves), thinly sliced
2 stalks bok choy, thinly sliced
Small piece of cabbage, thinly sliced
5 white mushrooms
2 shiitake mushrooms, thinly sliced
1-1/2 packages yakisoba noodles
2 cups spinach leaves
1/2 cup bean sprouts
1 carrot, shredded
24 egg roll wrappers

Combine onion, ginger, and garlic in a bowl and set aside. Thinly slice the Nappa, bok choy stalks, cabbage, as well as the mushrooms.

Give the yakisoba noodles a rough chop. Fry them in a tablespoon oil. After the noodles have fried in oil a bit and have browned, add a tablespoon of water, turn the heat to medium and put the lid on. After a couple of minutes the noodles will be easy to separate and will be soft. Remove the noodles from the pan and set aside.

Sauté the onions, ginger, and garlic in a tablespoon of oil. Add the mushrooms, bok choy & Nappa leaves. Stir and cook with the lid on for 2 minutes. Add the spinach, bean sprouts, carrots, and cabbage, etc. Cover and cook for 1 minute. Add the yakisoba noodles and yakisoba sauce packet. I used two sauce packages (it comes three noodle packages & 3 sauce packets in one bag of yakisoba).

(continued on the next page)

The seasoning packet, and traditional yakisoba sauce, is a sweet Worcestershire based sauce.

You can make it at home using 1 tablespoon each of mirin, vinegar, sake, oyster sauce, ketchup and brown sugar plus 2 tablespoons of Worcestershire sauce and shoyu. A half teaspoon of sriracha hot sauce is good in here, too.

Make the sauce in a bowl, then taste it and adjust the seasoning before you add it to the yakisoba. It's a lot easier than trying to adjust the flavors after it's already in the pan. Turn off the heat and stir well to combine all ingredients. When the mixture cools, place a small amount of the yakisoba onto an egg roll wrapper, close to one corner. Fold the wrapper in from the corner, tucking the corner under, press ends. Fold the right and left corners in. Moisten the top corner with a little bit of water so it will stick. Repeat until all wrappers are filled.

When the oil is hot, fry the egg roll until golden brown. You can tell when the oil is ready by putting a tiny bit of the egg roll noodle into the oil, when it sizzles, the oil is hot. Drain the egg roll on paper towels.

Thyra Abraham's Stuffed Sushi Cones

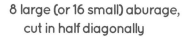

Thyra Abraham is my mom and is known to many as "Ma Abraham." She loves to cook and bake for other people, and I know that my passion for food and my passion for cooking comes from her. Thanks, Mom!

-Frank Abraham

8 large (or 16 small) aburage, cut in half diagonally

FILLING:

2 pounds ground beef
2 tablespoons mayonnaise
1 cup instant oatmeal (3 packets)
2 eggs
1/2 small carrot, grated
2 celery stalks, finely chopped
1/2 round onion, finely chopped
1 (8-ounce) can water chestnuts, drained and chopped
1 (5-ounce) can evaporated milk

SAUCE:

1 (24-ounce) bottle Del Monte ketchup (or your favorite brand)
1 can onion soup

Mix filling ingredients thoroughly and generously over-stuff each sushi cone (the aburage/sushi cones might need to be cut in half before stuffing). Place sauce ingredients into a non-stick pot and carefully place sushi cones face-down into sauce. Bring sauce to boil, then reduce heat to medium-low (to prevent burning) and cook for 45 to 60 minutes.

Frank Abraham's Shrimp, Edamame & Corn Tempura Fritters

Oil for frying

SHRIMP MIXTURE:

1 cup cleaned and chopped shrimp
1 cup cubed or shredded kamaboko
1 cup edamame (unshelled)
1 cup frozen corn, defrosted
1 tablespoon tempura flour
1 teaspoon salt
1/4 teaspoon pepper

BATTER:

2 egg yolks
1-1/2 cups ice water
1-3/4 cups sifted flour

TEMPURA DIPPING SAUCE:

1 cup dashi or 1 teaspoon instant dashi mixed with 1 cup water
2 teaspoons mirin
1 teaspoons Aloha Shoyu (soy sauce)

SHRIMP MIXTURE:

Prepare shrimp, kamaboko and vegetables and place in a bowl. Pat dry with paper towels. Add tempura flour, salt and pepper and coat mixture.

BATTER:

Put the egg yolks in a large bowl. Gradually add ice water, stirring and blending well. Add flour all at once, stir BRIEFLY (stir enough to coat, but leave the lumps).

Heat oil to 375°F. Add shrimp mixture to the tempura batter mixture. Avoid mixing too much. Drop mixture by tablespoonfuls into hot oil and cook until golden brown. Drain on paper towels. Serve with tempura dipping sauce.

TEMPURA DIPPING SAUCE:

Mix 1 cup of prepared dashi with mirin and shoyu. Heat over medium-high heat until warm. Serve warm.

CHAPTER 5

SWEETS

Wally Amos' Perfect Chocolate Chip Macadamia Cookies

ally Amos, probably one of the most famous and well-known cookie icons in the world, also happens to call Hawai'i home. I literally called Wally out of the blue to see if he would be interested in doing the show, not knowing what to expect. When I finally talked to him, he immediately said yes! He is such a gracious person who is generous with his time, and it was such a treat to meet and have him on the show. Currently, he has a new cookie venture in Hawai'i called The Cookie Kahuna. You can find more about him and his amazing cookies online at www.thecookiekahuna.com.

– Frank Abraham

1 pound butter or margarine (4 blocks)
4 eggs
2 teaspoons vanilla extract
2 teaspoons baking soda
1 teaspoon salt
1-1/2 cups light brown sugar
1-1/2 cups granulated sugar
4-1/2 cups all-purpose flour
8 ounces Island Princess Hawai'i
   macadamia nuts
36 ounces semi-sweet chocolate chips

Mix first 7 ingredients until thoroughly creamed. Add flour to creamed mixture slowly, a little at a time. Once batter is mixed, add macadamia nuts and chocolate chips. Be careful not to overmix batter to prevent batter from turning dark from the chocolate chips. Put batter in airtight container and chill overnight.

Preheat oven to 325°F. Cook on parchment paper or coated cookie sheet for about 10 minutes. Makes about 300 bite-sized cookies.

Hula Baby Biscotti's Papalua Fudge Cake with Mele Mac Coconut Swiss Meringue Buttercream

The folks at Hula Baby Biscotti and Kō Bakery on Kaua'i have been supporters of Cooking Hawaiian Style and the website since the very beginning. I love working with other companies from Hawai'i that share my passion for our food and culture. When asked to appear on the show, Morris and Chris jumped at the opportunity and decided to create a unique cake using products from Hawai'i. This is what they came up with. The cake has a big name and even bigger taste! It is honestly one of the best cakes that I have ever eaten! You can find out more about Hula Baby Biscotti and Kō Bakery and their artisan biscotti and baked goods by visiting their website at: www.papaluaisland.com.

– Frank Abraham

PAPALUA FUDGE CAKE:

2 cups all-purpose flour
1/2 teaspoon salt
1 teaspoon baking soda
1 cup organic coconut milk
1 tablespoon Kaua'i vanilla extract
1 tablespoon white distilled vinegar
3/4 cup cocoa powder
4-ounce block Hawaiian dark chocolate (semisweet or bittersweet), chopped
1/4 cup butter
1/2 cup water
4 egg whites
1 cup butter, softened
2 cups Maui white sugar
4 egg yolks

TOASTED COCONUT SWISS MERINGUE BUTTERCREAM :

1 (7-ounce) package Island Princess Hawai'i Mele Macs
1 cup organic unsweetened shredded coconut flakes
8 egg whites
2 cups sugar
1 pound plus 6 tablespoons unsalted butter, room temperature
1 tablespoon Kōloa Kaua'i coconut rum (optional)

PAPALUA FUDGE CAKE

1. Preheat oven to 350° F. Prepare three 8-inch cake pans by lining with parchment and coating with non-stick cooking spray.
2. Combine the flour, salt, and baking soda. Set aside.
3. Combine coconut milk, vanilla and vinegar. Set aside.
4. Combine cocoa, chopped chocolate, 1/4 cup butter and water in a small sauce pan and bring to simmer while stirring, remove from heat and cool.
5. Whip egg whites to stiff peaks in mixing bowl. Use a spatula to move whipped egg whites to another bowl and place in refrigerator until ready to use.
6. In the mixing bowl, cream the 1 cup softened butter and sugar well, until light and fluffy. Add yolks one at a time, beating well after each addition. Add cocoa mixture and mix well. Be sure to scrape down the bowl to incorporate all the ingredients.
7. Add flour mixture alternately with coconut milk mixture to chocolate batter, beating until smooth after each addition.
8. Gently fold whipped egg whites into the chocolate batter with a large silicone spatula. It helps to do one third of the whites at a time. Be sure there are no egg whites that aren't completely incorporated into the batter.

(continued on the next page)

9. Bake 20 to 30 minutes until cake tests done with a wooden toothpick or skewer.
10. Cool for 10 minutes in pans and then invert onto cooling racks. Finishing cooling to room temperature. Wrap each layer in plastic wrap and refrigerate until well chilled before handling and decorating.

FROSTING:

1. Reserve three or five whole Mele Macs and place the remainder in a storage bag and put in the freezer.
2. Spread the coconut flakes on a baking sheet and cook at 325°F until golden brown.
3. When the toasted coconut is completely cool, you may pulse in a food processor to a medium grain texture if necessary.
4. Separate your eggs making sure that there are no yolks.
5. Combine the egg whites and sugar in a metal bowl and whisk to combine.
6. Place the egg and sugar mixture over a pot of simmering water. Continue to whisk until the mixture registers 140°C on a candy thermometer.
7. Remove the whites and sugar from the heat and pour into your mixing bowl. Whip at high speed until stiff peaks are formed. Reduce to medium speed and continue whipping until the mixing bowl is completely cool to the touch.
8. Slowly add the room temperature butter a couple of tablespoons at a time. The buttercream may break (resembling soft cottage cheese). Continue to whip and the mixture will come back together.
9. Once all of the butter has been incorporated, add the coconut rum and toasted coconut. Stir with a rubber spatula for three to four minutes. This will help to remove some of the air from the buttercream, making it smoother.

ICING THE CAKE:

1. Remove the bag of Mele Macs from the freezer and pound with a heavy object such as a meat pounder or rolling pin to break up the candies into small pieces.
2. Use a serrated knife to trim the tops off each of the cake rounds. Place one of the rounds on your cake decorating turntable and spoon approximately 3/4 cup of the buttercream onto the middle of the cake round. Using an offset spatula spread the buttercream until it overhangs the edge of the cake just slightly. Sprinkle approximately half of the broken Mele Macs on the buttercream. Place the next layer on top, pressing down slightly, and repeat with the buttercream and the rest of the broken candy pieces.
3. Place the last layer of cake on top. Scoop a small amount of buttercream on the top. Finish the crumb coat on the cake by covering the entire thing in a light layer of buttercream. Don't worry if the frosting has cake crumbs in it, these won't be visible on the finished product.
4. Once the crumb coat is finished, place the cake in the refrigerator for 15 minutes.
5. Return the cake to your decorating turntable and scoop the remaining buttercream on top. This is the finishing layer of frosting, so go slowly and make the coverage as even as possible.
6. Place the reserved whole Mele Macs on the top of the cake to finish.
7. Cake can be decorated ahead and stored in the refrigerator. Remove from the refrigerator two to three hours before serving.

Frank Abraham's Chinese Rice Cake

1 cup long grain rice
1-1/2 cups water
1 cake compressed yeast *
1-1/2 cups sugar

* 1 cake of compressed yeast is just short of 1 ounce or 26 grams - substitute with just short of 1/2 ounce of dry active yeast or 11 to 12 grams.

Soak rice in water (have sufficient water to cover 1 inch above level of rice) for 2 days. Drain well. Mix compressed yeast with 1/2 cup lukewarm water. Add 1/4 cup sugar. Cover and set in warm place while you do the next step.

Put half of the soaked rice and 1/2 cup water into blender and blend at high speed until rice is liquefied and mixture is smooth (about 3 to 4 minutes). Set aside in mixing bowl. Blend remaining rice and water by 1/2 cup quantities, setting aside each portion into the same mixing bowl. Now pour the entire mixture back into blender and add 1-1/4 cups sugar. Blend at high speed for 2 more minutes.

Add yeast mixture and blend at low speed for 30 seconds. Pour into mixing bowl, cover and leave in a warm place until mixture is bubbly and almost double in bulk (about 1-1/2 to 2 hours).

STEAMING:

Start water in steamer boiling. Lightly stir batter again to mix evenly. Pour batter into round or square cake pan to about 1/2-inch high. Steam for 12 to 15 minutes. Cool completely. Lightly rub a little oil on top to give it a glossy appearance. Cut into diamond shapes. Rice cake is eaten when it is at room temperature.

Note: The rice needs to be soaked for 2 days so it will be easily liquefied. The fermenting process is extremely important, so don't rush it. The textural appearance in the cross section of the rice cake should be full of holes (air pockets) throughout.

Frank Abraham's Island Princess Hawai'i Mele Mac & Macadamia Nut Pie

3 eggs
2/3 cup sugar
1 cup light corn syrup
2 cups Island Princess Hawai'i Mele Macs
1 cup Island Princess Hawai'i macadamia nut halves, salted
3 tablespoons butter, melted
2 tablespoons cream
1 teaspoon vanilla
1 unbaked 9-inch pie shell

Beat eggs with sugar and corn syrup. Add butter, cream and vanilla and blend well. Place mele macs into empty pie shell followed by macadamia nuts. Pour mixture into pie shell. Bake at 325°F for 50 minutes or until the crust is golden and the center is somewhat set. Let the pie cool and chill.

Note: The pie should be fairly runny when hot and the mele macs should melt into the pie. Once it cools, it will set. You can also refrigerate it for 15 to 20 minutes before serving with a huge dollop of whipped cream!

Island Princess Hawai'i
Mini Mele Peanut Butter Cookies

Yolanda and Island Princess Hawai'i was the first company to support my efforts in creating the website and continue to support anything and everything that we do. Nothing makes me happier than working with local Hawai'i companies that are producing products using ingredients from Hawai'i. The folks at Island Princess Hawai'i have bent over backwards to support me and *Cooking Hawaiian Style*, and Yolanda, head of Marketing, is like a sister to me. For me, this is what *Cooking Hawaiian Style* is all about– fellowship, sharing and spreading aloha. Find out more about Island Princess Hawai'i and all of their made-in-Hawai'i products at: www.islandprincesshawaii.com.

– Frank Abraham

1-1/2 cup sugar
1 cup butter-flavored all-vegetable shortening plus extra for greasing pan
1 cup creamy peanut butter
3 eggs
3 cups all-purpose flour
1/2 teaspoon salt
1 tablespoon cream of tartar
1 teaspoon baking soda
Island Princess Hawai'i Mini Meles™ (about 4 [2.5-ounce] bags or 1-1/2 [5-ounce] jar of Mini Meles*)

Preheat oven to 375°F. Combine sugar and shortening in large bowl. With an electric mixer, mix at medium speed until blended well. Beat in peanut butter and eggs. In separate bowl, mix together the dry ingredients: flour, salt, cream of tartar, and baking soda. Add gradually to creamed mixture at low speed and mix until well blended. Grease baking sheet with left-over shortening. Shape dough into 1-1/4-inch balls, place 2 inches apart on greased baking sheet. Press tip of your finger halfway down in center of dough ball (do not flatten). Lightly place one Island Princess Hawai'i Mini Mele piece into impression.

Bake at 375° F for 9 to 11 minutes or until light brown. Remove from oven. Cool 3 minutes on baking sheet before moving cookies to cooling rack. Makes about 4-1/2 dozen cookies.

Note: There are about 8 Mini Mele pieces per ounce, size varies by the size of the macadamia nut halves in each piece

THYRA ABRAHAM'S CHOCOLATE HAUPIA PIE

MACADAMIA NUT SHORTBREAD CRUST:

1 cup Island Princess Hawai'i unsalted macadamia nuts
1 cup all purpose flour
4 tablespoons rice flour
4 tablespoons sugar
4 tablespoons dark brown sugar
1 teaspoon salt
8 tablespoons cold unsalted butter, cut into 1/4-inch cubes
2 tablespoons cold milk
1/2 teaspoon vanilla extract

1 (14-ounce) can coconut milk
1 cup milk
1 cup white sugar
1/2 cup cornstarch
1 cup water
1 cup semisweet chocolate chips
1-1/2 cups heavy cream
1/4 cup white sugar

CRUST:

Preheat oven to 325°F. Coat pie pan with cooking spray. Toast macadamia nuts in shallow pan for 5 minutes or until golden brown. Place toasted macadamia nuts in food processor, add dry ingredients and pulse until a fine meal is achieved. Add cold butter a little at a time and continue pulsing in processor. Add milk and vanilla and pulse. Crust will slowly start to form and pull away from the sides. Remove crust and press into pie pan. Bake for 25 to 35 minutes. Cool thoroughly before using.

next time, use spring form pan

FILLING:

In a medium pan, add coconut milk, milk, sugar and whisk. In separate bowl, whisk cornstarch and water until smooth. Over medium-high heat, cook milk mixture stirring constantly until it reaches a boil. Turn heat down to simmer and slowly add cornstarch mixture whisking constantly for three minutes until mixture thickens. In a microwave safe bowl, melt chocolate in microwave for 1 minute. Stir, then repeat in microwave a minute at a time until chocolate is completely melted and smooth (2 to 3 minutes). Separate the coconut pudding mixture into two equal portions. Add melted chocolate to one of the puddings and stir until entirely mixed. Pour chocolate coconut pudding mixture into pie crust and allow to cool for 5 to 10 minutes. Once set, pour coconut pudding mixture over the chocolate coconut pudding mixture. Refrigerate for 2 hours. In a cold bowl, whip heavy whipping cream and sugar until soft peaks form. Serve pie and garnish with whipped cream.

3/20'w Powers from Py.

Malika Dudley's Macadamia Nut Crêpes

1 cup flour
1/2 cup sugar
3 eggs
2 tablespoons oil
1 teaspoon vanilla
1-1/2 cups milk
Couple splashes of beer (optional)
Butter, to grease pan

Fillings: Macadamia Nuts, whipped cream, yogurt, fresh fruit, preserves... whatever you prefer!

Add ingredients together (except butter). Whisk together until smooth. Let rest with a dish cloth over it out on the counter. Let crêpe pan get really hot (don't be afraid if it starts smoking). Use a stick of butter to butter the pan. (Keep the butter out as it's used for each crêpe.) I usually take the pan off the heat to do this.

Use a soup ladle to put crêpe batter into pan. You want the batter to be enough to cover the pan but not too thick. Figure out how far up in the ladle is the perfect amount of batter for your pan and repeat. (This may take a few tries and you almost always ruin your first crêpe—don't worry, it still tastes good!) Once you see bubbles and/or the crêpe is just cooked enough to flip, then flip the crêpe. Remove when golden brown. Add fillings of your choice! Voila!

Thyra Abraham's Liliko'i Chiffon Pie

4 egg yolks (save whites)
1/3 cup white sugar
1/2 teaspoon salt
1/2 cup passion fruit drink (we use undiluted concentrate)
1 tablespoon unflavored gelatin
1/4 cup cold water
2 teaspoons grated lemon zest
4 egg whites
1 cup white sugar
6 to 8 drops of yellow food coloring (optional)
9-inch prepared graham cracker crust (recipe follows)
Whipped cream (recipe follows)

CRUST:

1-1/4 cups graham cracker crumbs (about 15 graham crackers)
1/4 cup sugar
1/3 cup melted butter

STABILIZED WHIPPED CREAM:

1/2 teaspoon unflavored gelatin
1 tablespoon water
1 cup whipping cream
1/2 teaspoon vanilla
2 tablespoons powdered sugar, or to taste

In a double boiler, combine egg yolks, 1/3 cup sugar, salt and passion fruit concentrate. Cook over low heat, stirring constantly, until thickened. Dissolve gelatin in cold water, then stir into yolk mixture. Stir in lemon zest. Remove from heat and allow to cool until slightly congealed.

In a large glass or metal mixing bowl, beat egg whites until foamy. Gradually add 1 cup white sugar, continuing to beat until stiff peaks form. Gently fold whites into yolk mixture until no streaks remain. Stir in food coloring, if desired. Spoon into pie crust. Refrigerate for 2 hours, or until firm. Top with whipped cream.

CRUST:

Preheat oven to 375°F. Crumble graham crackers into food processor fitted with metal chopping blade and churn 30 seconds. Add sugar and butter and pulse 30 seconds until uniformly fine. Press crumb mixture into pie plate as directed. Bake 8 to 10 minutes. Makes one 9-inch pie shell.

STABILIZED WHIPPED CREAM:

Dissolve gelatin in water. Whip cream until soft peaks form; add gelatin and continue beating until cream is stiff. If desired, add vanilla and powdered sugar. Whipped cream will hold for 24 hours in the refrigerator.

Lori Ikeda's
Guava Cream Cheese Custard Rolls

3 dozen King's Hawaiian Sweet Rolls

CREAM CHEESE CUSTARD:

4 ounces cream cheese
1-1/2 cups milk
6 tablespoons sugar
1/8 teaspoon salt
1 egg yolk
2 tablespoons cornstarch
1-1/2 teaspoons butter
1 teaspoon vanilla extract

TOPPING:

3/4 cup frozen guava juice concentrate, thawed
2-1/4 teaspoons cornstarch

Place rolls on large baking sheets. Use a small paring knife to cut a cone-shaped piece out of the top of each roll, going a little past halfway deep. This creates a well for the custard filling. Set aside the cut outs for another use.

Place all the custard ingredients except for the butter and vanilla into a blender. Blend for 30 to 60 seconds until all the ingredients are well incorporated. Pour into a saucepan and cook on medium-high heat, whisking frequently until the mixture is thickened and starts to bubble. Lower heat to medium, cook and whisk another 2 minutes. Don't let the bottom burn. Remove from heat. Whisk in butter, until it is melted, then the vanilla. Pour into a bowl and cool 5 minutes. Spoon 1 tablespoon custard into each roll. Cover rolls with plastic wrap and place in the refrigerator.

For the topping, pour guava juice concentrate into a small saucepan. Whisk in cornstarch until there are no lumps. Cook over medium-high heat, whisking frequently until it is thickened and bubbling. Allow to cook 30 to 60 seconds more, then pour into a shallow bowl and cool to room temperature. Spoon 1 teaspoon topping onto the top of each roll. Place rolls in airtight containers (like large, rectangular plastic containers with lids) and chill.

The topping will take a couple of hours to gel firm, but these can be eaten immediately. Keep tightly covered in the refrigerator to keep rolls soft. They can also be heated in the microwave for a few seconds to warm if desired, or soften if needed.

Chris Souza's Crisp Coconut Cookies

1 cup butter or margarine
1 cup sugar
1 teaspoon vanilla
2 cups flour
1-1/3 cups shredded coconut

Preheat oven to 300°F. In a large bowl of electric mixer, cream butter and sugar. Add vanilla and beat thoroughly. Slowly mix in flour and coconut and mix well. Shape into balls the size of walnuts. Place on ungreased baking sheets and flatten with the bottom of a glass dipped in flour. Bake for 20 to 25 minutes. Makes 4 dozen.

PATRICIA ANDERSON'S APRICOT TURNOVERS

Pat is one of my mom's best friends and has a treasure trove of recipes including old newspaper clippings of a Zippy's chili recipe and a Leonard's malasada recipe. This particular recipe was given to her by the baker at the original Tropic Bakery on 12th Avenue in Kaimuki.

– Frank Abraham

4 cups flour
1-1/2 cups vegetable shortening
10 ounces cream cheese
Pinch of salt
Apricot jam
Powdered sugar

Cream first 4 ingredients until well blended. Roll into ball. Roll out and cut with round cookie cutter. Place 1 teaspoon jam in center and fold in half. Seal edges. Place on cookie sheet and bake at 325°F until light brown. Remove from cookie sheet and sprinkle with powdered sugar.

Frank Abraham's Taro Chip Cookies

1/2 cup shortening
1/2 cup butter
1 cup sugar
1 cup light brown sugar
2 eggs, room temperature
2 cups sifted flour
1 teaspoon salt
1 teaspoon baking soda
1 teaspoon vanilla
2 cups f finely crushed ried taro chips
1 cup Island Princess Hawai'i macadamia nuts, chopped

Preheat oven 325°F. In a large mixing bowl, cream together shortening, butter, and both sugars. Add eggs and mix well.

In a separate bowl, mix together flour, salt and baking soda and gradually add to butter-sugar mixture. Next, add vanilla and fold in crushed chips and nuts. Shape into small balls and place on ungreased cookie sheet. Gently flatten cookie dough with a fork or bottom of a glass. Bake for 10 to 15 minutes. Cool for 5 minutes, then allow to cool on brown paper or paper towels.

BETTY SHIMABUKURO'S CROCKPOT COCONUT TAPIOCA

1/2 cup small pearl tapioca
(sold in Asian markets)
3 cups water
Pinch salt
1 (13-ounce) can coconut milk
1/2 cup sugar
1 teaspoon vanilla extract
1/4 cup passion fruit juice
1 cup chopped fruit (mango,
banana, strawberries,
honeydew melon, kiwi or
lychee are all good)

Place tapioca pearls and water in 2-quart slow-cooker. Add salt. Cook on high until pearls turn from white to translucent, 2 to 3 hours. Don't be concerned if nothing seems to be happening for the first hour. The heat has to rise enough for the water to simmer.

Mixture will be thick and sticky; stir well, then add coconut milk and sugar. (If coconut milk has been chilled, warm in microwave before adding.) Stir until sugar dissolves. Add vanilla. Taste, adding more sugar if necessary. Divide among 8 dessert cups. Chill until firm. Pour a thin layer of juice over each cup of pudding. Top with fruit.

Frank Abraham's Kona Coffee Macadamia Brittle

Nonstick cooking spray

COFFEE MIXTURE:

1 tablespoon freeze-dried Kona
    coffee granules
1 teaspoon baking soda
1/4 teaspoon kosher salt

1 cup granulated sugar
1/4 cup water
1/4 teaspoon cream of tartar
2 tablespoons butter
1 cup rough chopped Island
    Princess Hawai'i macadamia nuts

Spray a baking sheet with nonstick cooking spray. Combine coffee granules, baking soda and salt in small bowl; set aside.

Combine sugar, water and cream of tartar in medium, heavy-duty saucepan. Stir with wooden spoon over low heat until sugar is dissolved, occasionally scraping sides of pan with spatula. Once sugar is melted, bring to a boil over medium-high heat. Continue cooking for about 6 minutes stirring occassionally until mixture is a light brown color. Remove from heat and add butter and coffee mixture and stir mixture as it bubbles and foams. Add macadamia nuts and mix thoroughly.

Pour mixture onto baking sheet and spread mixture evenly. Allow brittle to continue cooling for 30 minutes, break into pieces and store in a cool place in an airtight container.

Thyra Abraham's
Fresh Mango & Jello Cheesecake

1-1/2 cups flour
1/2 cup powdered sugar
3/4 cup butter
1/2 cup Island Princess Hawai'i macadamia nuts, coarsely chopped
8-ounces cream cheese, softened
1/2 cup sugar
1 teaspoon vanilla
1 (8-ounce) container frozen whipped topping, thawed
1 (6-ounce) package orange flavored gelatin
3 cups boiling water
4 cups mangoes, diced

Preheat oven to 350°F. In bowl, combine flour and powdered sugar, cut in butter. Mix in nuts. Lightly press into a 13 x 9-inch pan. Bake 15 minutes.

In large bowl, beat cream cheese, sugar and vanilla. Gently fold in whipped topping. Spread over cooled crust, chill until firm (at least 1 to 2 hours).

Dissolve gelatin in boiling water, cool. Arrange mangoes over cream cheese layer. Pour cooled gelatin over mangoes. Chill until firm. Cut into squares. Serves 24.

OOKING
HAWAII

CHAPTER 6

CHEFS' SPECIALS

Chef Nicole LaTorre's 'Ahi Carpaccio

AIOLI:

Juice of 1 lemon
5 fresh garlic cloves, finely minced
1/2 to 3/4 cup mayonnaise
Salt & pepper to taste

1 pound fresh 'ahi tuna
Plastic wrap (or wax paper)
Pickled ginger (garnish)
Lemon and lime wedges (garnish)
Avocado slices (garnish)

Prepare aioli by mixing juice of 1 lemon and 5 cloves of minced garlic. Add mayonnaise, salt and pepper to taste. Mix well and pour mixture into a plastic squirt bottle and set aside in refrigerator.

Slice 'ahi with the grain of the fish. Take pieces of fish and place between two pieces of plastic wrap. Using a meat pounder or other smooth heavy object, gently flatten the fish fillets until nice and thin. Place carpaccio on serving platter, garnish with ginger, lemon and lime wedges. Squirt aioli over carpaccio and top with avocado slices.

Chef Adam Tabura's Steamed 'Ōpakapaka

2 to 3 ti leaves
2 (6-ounce) 'ōpakapaka fillets
2 cloves garlic, smashed
1/4 cup peanut oil

SWEET SOY REDUCTION:

1 cup sweet soy sauce
2 tablespoons mirin
1/2 teaspoon grated ginger (or to taste)
1 clove garlic, crushed

GARNISH:

1 block tofu, sliced 1/4-inch thin
8 to 10 sprigs cilantro
1 carrot, julienned
1/4 red bell pepper, julienned
8 green onions, cut into 4-inch pieces

Boil water in a pot and place bamboo steamer basket lined with ti leaves over top of pot. Place fish fillets on ti leaves and steam for 10 to 15 minutes.

SWEET SOY REDUCTION:

Add sweet soy sauce, mirin, grated ginger and garlic to small pot and cook over medium-high heat for a couple minutes. Reduce heat to medium and allow soy sauce to reduce or evaporate until only 1/2 cup remains. Set aside and allow to cool in pan.

GARNISH:

Take tofu and cut entire block into 1/4-inch slices. Wash and rinse 8 to 10 sprigs of cilantro and set aside. Julienne carrot and red bell pepper and set aside. Cut green onion into 4-inch pieces using both the white stem and the green leaf.

HOT OIL:

Heat peanut oil in a small pan and add crushed garlic. Heat on medium-high heat until oil is hot and garlic is aromatic. Do not overheat and burn garlic. Set aside and assemble dish.

ASSEMBLE:

Place thin slice of tofu on plate. Add a layer of julienned carrots and 2 green onion leaves. Gently place fish fillet on top of tofu and carrots. Top fish fillet with 2 green onion leaves, bell pepper and cilantro. Pour about 2 tablespoons of hot oil over vegetables to release aromatics. Glaze with 2 to 4 tablespoons of the soy reduction.

CHEF ADAM TABURA'S 'ŌPAKAPAKA SASHIMI

4 ounces fresh 'ōpakapaka, sliced sashimi-style
1 tomato, diced

DRESSING:

1 teaspoon sesame oil
1 teaspoon peanut oil
Pinch Hawaiian salt

Dash sweet chili oil
2 fresh garlic cloves, minced
4 to 6 green onions, sliced

Slice fish sashimi style, sprinkle tomatoes on fish. Make dressing by mixing oils and Hawaiian salt. Top sashimi with dressing and sweet chili oil, fresh garlic and green onions.

Chef Adam Tabura's 'Ōpakapaka Soup

BASIC BROTH:

6 cups water
Leftover fish bones, skin etc.
1 stalk lemon grass, crushed
1 bay leaf
2 tablespoons vinegar
2 tablespoons salt
Pepper
Black peppercorns
1 piece ginger
Lemon/lime slices

IN SOUP BOWL:

2 ounces fresh snapper, thinly sliced
1 piece lemon grass
Handful tomatoes, chopped
Handful cilantro
Handful tofu, diced
Green onions, sliced
Ginger, minced
Garlic, minced
Chili pepper/Jalapeño
Fresh lemon
Chili paste

BROTH:

Bring water to boil. Put all ingredients in cheesecloth and wrap. Add cheesecloth to pot, allow to simmer for 30 to 45 minutes. Discard contents of cheesecloth.

SERVING:

Build each soup bowl by putting a little bit of each ingredient into bowl, then top with hot broth. The fish and aromatic vegetables will cook to perfection from the heat of the broth. Season with salt if necessary.

Chef Adam Tabura's Braised Beef Brisket Loco Moco

1 pound beef brisket
Salt & pepper to taste
1/2 cup beef demiglace
1 Hawaiian chili pepper, chopped
Boiling water + 1 tablespoon vinegar
Cooked rice
6 duck eggs

Preheat oven to 325°F. Season brisket with salt and pepper. Put beef brisket in small roasting pan with about 1/4 cup water. Cover with foil and bake for 2 hours. Remove brisket from oven and allow to cool for 10 minutes. Place drippings in small pot and add 1/2 cup demiglace to the drippings. If more liquid is needed, use beef broth as necessary. Season gravy if necessary with salt and pepper and add chopped Hawaiian chili pepper to taste.

In a small pot, boil water and add 1 tablespoon vinegar. Reduce heat to a low simmer. One at a time, break eggs into a bowl and from the bowl, gently release eggs into simmering water. Do not allow the water to boil. Cook for 1 to 2 minutes. Meanwhile, put a portion of rice on plate or in bowl, slice a piece of brisket and layer over rice, put poached egg on the top and cover with brown gravy.

CHEF MAVRO'S SALT CRUSTED ONAGA WITH FRESH OGO SAUCE

I was honored to have Chef Mavro grace us with his culinary expertise. Recipient of the prestigious James Beard Award, Chef's talent was apparent from start to end. I met Chef Mavro many times but having him next to me and watching him work was a real treat. He made us one of his signature dishes and now you get to try it!

-Lanai Tabura

SALT CRUST DOUGH:

2 pounds flour (all-purpose)
1 pound rock salt
1 tablespoon dry rosemary
1 tablespoon dry thyme
3 egg whites
1 cup water

FISH:

1 whole onaga
   (long tail red snapper, 2 pounds)
1 pound spinach leaves
3 garlic cloves, finely chopped
3 tablespoons olive oil
2 large ti leaves

FRESH OGO SAUCE:

2 shallots, finely chopped
6 tablespoons olive oil
3 garlic cloves, finely chopped
1/2 cup white wine
1 tomato, peeled, seeded, diced
1 sprig tarragon, finely chopped
1 sprig chervil, finely chopped
2 tablespoons finely chopped
   green onions
1/2 cup ogo (Hawaiian seaweed),
   finely chopped
Salt & pepper to taste

METHOD FOR THE DOUGH:

Sieve the flour into a mixing bowl. Add the rock salt, rosemary, thyme and eggs with half a cup of water. Mix until a stiff dough is formed with the remainder of the water. Roll out the dough to get enough to wrap the fish.

METHOD FOR THE FISH:

Ask your butcher to remove the fillets from the onaga keeping the skin on. Sauté the spinach with garlic and 3 tablespoons of olive oil. Season to taste and cool in the refrigerator for a few minutes. Put the ti leaves on the dough to protect the fish from the salt (the top of the fish will be protected by the skin). Arrange the spinach on the ti leaves with the two fillets skin up (laying side by side) on the top of spinach. Wrap the onaga in the rock salt dough and shape the dough like a fish. Bake in the oven for 25 minutes at 375°F.

METHOD FOR THE SAUCE:

In a sauce pan sauté the shallots in 4 tablespoons olive oil for a few minutes (do not color the shallots). Add the garlic and white wine, and reduce to half. Add all the other ingredients. Finish with remaining olive oil. Season to taste.

TO SERVE:

At tableside cut the crust lengthwise, removing only the top of the crust. (Extra caution should be taken so that no salt crystals fall onto the fish). Remove the skin from the fish. On individual plates, place the spinach on top of the fish and arrange the sauce around the fish.

GLOSSARY

Aburage: Japanese name for deep-fried tofu

Achiote seeds: seeds from lipstick plant; also known as annatto or achuete

'Ahi: Hawaiian name for yellowfin tuna

Aioli: garlic mayonnaise

Béchamel sauce: a white sauce made with a roux of butter and flour cooked in milk

Bitter melon: an oblong, extremely bitter fruit, widely grown in Asia, Africa, and the Caribbean; known in Okinawan cooking as goya

Bok choy: type of cabbage used in Chinese cuisine

Char siu pork: Chinese sweet roasted pork

Chimichurri: green sauce originally from Argentina made with parsley, garlic, olive oil, oregano, and red or white wine vinegar

Chinese five spice: blend of star anise, cloves, fennel, peppercorns, and cinnamon

Dashi: Japanese term for broth

Gochujang—Korean chili paste which may contain black beans, garlic, and spices; also spelled kochujang

Haupia: Hawaiian coconut pudding

Hawaiian salt: coarse sea salt; rock salt

Hoisin: Chinese soybean sauce used as a condiment or for flavoring

Kamaboko: Japanese steamed fish cake

Koena: outer layer of taro scrapings

Lechon kawali: fried pork belly

Longanisa sausage: Filipino pork sausage

Lū'au leaves: taro leaves

Mochiko: rice flour

Nori: dried laver; seaweed

Ogo: Japanese term for seaweed

Onaga: Japanese term for red snapper

Ong choi: also known as water spinach, it grows in tropical and subtropical regions and is a common ingredient in Southeast Asian cuisines

'Ōpakapaka: Hawaiian for pink snapper

Opu: long squash

Pa'i 'ai: hard, pounded but undiluted taro

Panko: Japanese style bread crumbs

Patis: Filipino fish sauce

Poi: Hawaiian staple; starchy paste made from mashed taro

Shoga: fresh ginger root

Sriracha: U.S.-made hot sauce from sun-ripened chili peppers, vinegar, garlic, sugar, and salt, similar to the hot sauces of Vietnam and Thailand

Tako: Japanese word for octopus

Truffle oil: popular with modern chefs because it's less expensive than actual truffles, it has an olive oil or grapeseed oil base combined with an odorant found in truffles

RECIPE INDEX

A

Amy Kristy's Spam Quiche, 13
Augie T's Corned Beef & Cabbage, 3
Aunty Bea Rodrigues' Pastele Stew, 16

B

Betty Shimabukuro's Crockpot Coconut Tapioca, 105
Betty Shimabukuro's Ramen Burger, 64

C

Caroline Hoke's (Caroline's Creations) Parmesan Garlic Wings, 6
Chef Adam Tabura's 'Ōpakapaka Sashimi, 114
Chef Adam Tabura's 'Ōpakapaka Soup, 117
Chef Adam Tabura's Steamed 'Ōpakapaka, 113
Chef Adam Tabura's Braised Beef Brisket Loco Moco, 118
Chef Ippy Aiona's Beef Steak Tataki, 39
Chef Ippy Aiona's Pork Belly Adobo, 36
Chef Mavro's Salt Crusted Onaga with Fresh Ogo Sauce, 121
Chef Nicole Latorre's 'Ahi Carpaccio, 110
Chris Souza's Crisp Coconut Cookies, 102
Chris Souza's Okazuya-Style Chow Fun, 26
Colleen Hanabusa's Clam Pasta, 48
Colleen Hanabusa's Fresh 'Ahi Pasta, 46

D

Daniel Anthony's Instant Pa'i 'Ai Kulolo, 42
Daniel Anthony's Koena Meatloaf, 43
David Ryusaki's Tater Tot Casserole, 5

Deirdre Todd's Hanamā'ulu-Style Shrimp, 30
Deirdre Todd's Char Siu Gin Doi, 53
Deirdre Todd's Mai Tai Soo (Chop Suey Cake), 31

E

Elena's Restaurant Sari Sari, 18

F

Frank Abraham's Chinese Rice Cake, 90
Frank Abraham's Chinese Roast Style Fried Chicken, 34
Frank Abraham's Crispy Gau Gee (Wontons), 27
Frank Abraham's Hamburger Curry, 33
Frank Abraham's Island Princess Hawai'i Mele Mac & Macadamia Nut Pie, 91
Frank Abraham's Kālua Lū'au Lasagna Rolls With Haupia Béchamel Sauce, 69
Frank Abraham's Killer Brown Gravy, 32
Frank Abraham's Shrimp, Edamame & Corn Tempura Fritters, 80
Frank Abraham's Taro Chip Cookies, 104
Frank Abraham's Teriyaki Chicken Skewers with Fresh Tomato Chimichurri, 70
Frank Abraham's Kamaboko Omelette, 12
Frank Abraham's Kona Coffee Macadamia Brittle, 106

G

Glen Shinsato's Cured Pork Chop with Arugula Butter, 67

Glen Shinsato's Cured Pork Patty Sandwich, 66

H

Hula Baby Biscotti's Papalua Fudge Cake With Mele Mac Coconut Swiss Meringue Buttercream, 86

I

Island Princess Hawai'i Mini Mele Peanut Butter Cookies, 92

K

Kaleo Pilanca's Hamburger Watercress with Chomorro Ribs & Finadene Sauce, 44

Karolyn Fujimoto's Yakisoba Egg Rolls, 77

Kimi Werner's Smoked 'Ahi Pizza, 56

L

Lanai Tabura's Crescent Roll Lasagna, 10

Lanai Tabura's Hamburger Broccoli, 10

Lanai Tabura's Mom's Pinakbet, 52

Lanai's Snapper Egg Foo Young, 72

Lori Ikeda's Green Onion And Chili Oil Pa'i 'Ai Biscuits, 74

Lori Ikeda's Guava Cream Cheese Custard Rolls, 100

Lori Ikeda's Pa'i 'Ai Crackers, 76

M

Mahealani Richardson's Swamp Juice, 4

Mahealani Richardson's Oscar The Grouch Applesauce, 4

Malika Dudley's Couscous, 8

Malika Dudley's Macadamia Nut Crêpes, 97

Melveen Leed's Crustacean Polynesia, 49

Mom Tabura's Spaghettini Crab Salad, 25

O

Olena Heu's Bombucha Salad With Seared Poke & Liliko'i Vinaigrette, 60

Onda Pasta's Kahuku Shrimp & Fresh Pasta, 58

P

Patricia Anderson's Apricot Turnovers, 103

Popo June Tong's Pork Hash, 50

Popo June Tong's Shrimp Toast, 51

R

Radasha Ho'ohuli's Pork & Beans with Hot Dogs, 2

Raiatea Helms' Chicken Lū'au Stew, 24

Raiatea Helms' Kahuku Style Garlic Shimp, 22

Raymond Noh's Kim Chee Steak, 63

Raymond Noh's Poke Trio, 62

S

Sai Kairod's Cilantro Chili Chicken Skewers, 73

Senator Daniel Inouye's Sweet & Sour Spare Ribs, 35

Sid Alapai's Adobo Fried Chicken, 68

Sid Alapai's Macadamia Nut Hummus, 11

Sugoi's Hawai'i Garlic Furikake Chicken, 28

Sugoi's Hawai'i Teri Loco Moco, 29

T

Thyra Abraham's Chocolate Haupia Pie, 94

Thyra Abraham's Fresh Mango & Jello Cheesecake, 107

Thyra Abraham's Liliko'i Chiffon Pie, 98

Thyra Abraham's Stuffed Sushi Cones, 79

Titus Chan's Pork Chow Mein (Gravy Noodles), 21

W

Wally Amos' Perfect Chocolate Chip Macadamia Cookies, 85

Index

A

aburage, 79
achiote seeds, 16
'ahi, 46, 56, 58, 60-62, 110
aioli, 39, 110
apple cider vinegar, 6, 36
apricot jam, 103
arugula, 56, 58, 65, 67
avocado, 110

B

balsamic reduction, 56, 58
bean sprouts, 26, 72, 77
béchamel sauce, 56, 58
beef brisket, 118
bittermelon, 52
bok choy, 77
brown gravy, 29, 32, 118

C

cabbage, 3, 77
capers, 46
char siu, 26
Cheddar cheese, 5, 10, 13
chia flat bread, 56
chicken, 5-6, 21-22, 24, 28, 34, 44-45, 65, 68, 70-71, 73
chicken wings, 6
chimichurri, 70-71
Chinese five spice, 35
cilantro, 8, 16, 18, 21, 51, 60, 70-71, 73, 113-114, 117
Chinese roast pork, 31
chow fun, 26
chow mein, 21
clams, 48-49
cocoa powder, 86

coconut milk, 36, 42, 49, 69, 86-87, 94-95, 105
compressed yeast, 90
cornstarch, 21, 24, 30, 50-51, 68, 70-71, 94-95, 100-101
corned beef, 3
couscous, 8-9
crabmeat, 25
cream cheese, 100, 103, 107
curry powder, 33

D

dashi, 27, 80-81
demiglace, 118
duck eggs, 118

E

edamame, 7, 80
eggplant, 18, 52
evaporated milk, 33, 79

F

finadene sauce, 44-45
fried taro chips, 104

G

garbanzo beans, 11
garlic, 6-8, 10-11, 13, 16, 18, 21-22, 24, 28-29, 35-36, 44-46, 52, 56, 58-59, 66-68, 70-71, 73, 77, 110, 113-114, 117, 121-122
ginger, 18, 24, 26, 30, 35, 46, 52, 70, 72, 77, 110, 113, 117
gochujang, 7
green onion, 12, 26, 31, 44, 53, 65, 74, 113-114
ground pork, 27, 29, 50-51, 66
ground beef, 5, 10, 29, 33, 43-45, 64, 79
guava juice concentrate, 100-101

H

Hāmākua mushrooms, 56
hamburger, 10, 32-33, 44-45, 65
haupia, 69, 94
Hawaiian chili pepper, 60, 71, 118
Hawaiian salt, 18, 43, 63, 114
hoisin, 53, 72, 123
honey, 60, 72
hot dogs, 2

I

Island Princess Hawai'i Mele Macs, 86, 91
Island Princess Hawai'i Mini Meles, 92

J

Jello, 107

K

kālua pork, 65, 69
kamaboko, 12, 80
King's Hawaiian Sweet Rolls, 100
koena, 42-43

L

lasagna, 10, 69
lechon kawali (fried pork belly), 18
light corn syrup, 91
liliko'i, 60, 98
linguine, 46, 48
longanisa sausage, 52
lū'au leaves, 24, 69

M

macadamia nuts, 11, 60, 85, 91, 94, 97, 104, 106-107
mango, 105, 107
Maui onion, 46, 49, 56
mayonnaise, 6, 25, 39, 79, 110
mochiko flour, 28, 53
Morton Tender Quick, 66-67

N

Noh Chinese roast chicken seasoning, 34
Noh Hawaiian hot sauce, 62
Noh kim chee seasoning, 63
Noh poke seasoning, 60
nori, 46

O

ogo, 61-62, 121
okra, 52
olive oil, 6, 8, 10-11, 46, 48, 58, 60, 70-71, 73, 121-122
onaga, 44, 121-122
ong choi, 18
'ōpakapaka, 113-114, 117
opu, 18
oyster sauce, 3, 12, 21, 26-27, 30, 72, 78

P

pa'i 'ai, 42-43, 74-76
panko, 29
Parmesan cheese, 6, 13, 48, 56, 58
parsley, 8, 25, 46, 48, 51, 58-59, 70-71
passion fruit juice, 60, 105
patis, 18-19, 52
peanut oil, 113-114
peppercorns, 36, 63, 68, 117
pickled ginger, 110
poi, 124
poke, 60-62
pork & beans, 2, 18, 52
pork belly, 18, 36
pork butt, 16
pork spare ribs, 35
pumpkin, 52

R

ramen, 64
raw sugar, 42
rice, 12, 28-29, 31, 45, 53, 60, 90, 94, 118
rice wine vinegar, 31, 60

S

sake, 46, 78
salmon, 62
sesame oil, 7, 21, 27, 30, 50, 53, 60-62, 72, 114
sesame seeds, 31, 46, 53
shiitake mushrooms, 31, 77
shoga ginger, 46, 124
shoyu (soy sauce), 3, 12, 26-28, 30-33, 36, 44-45, 62, 68, 70, 78, 80-81
shredded coconut, 86, 102
shrimp, 18-19, 22, 27, 30-31, 49-51, 53, 58-59, 80-81

smoked 'ahi, 56
snapper, 72, 117, 121
soy sauce, 3, 12, 21, 26-27, 30-33, 35-36,
    44-45, 50, 68, 70, 80, 113
spaghettini, 25
Spam, 13
sriracha, 31, 78
string beans, 52
sweet chili sauce, 73

T

tako, 62, 124
tapioca, 64, 105
tater tots, 5
teriyaki sauce, 28-29
tofu, 72, 113-114, 117
tomatoes, 8, 18, 52, 58-59, 71-72, 114, 117
truffle oil, 56, 58

V

vanilla, 85-87, 91, 94, 97, 99-100, 102,
    104-105, 107
vegetable shortening, 103

W

wasabi, 31
watercress, 44-45, 127
water chestnuts, 31, 51, 79
wondra flour, 32
wonton chips, 60-61
wonton wrappers, 27

Y

yakisoba, 77-78

ABOUT THE AUTHORS

FRANK ABRAHAM
Owner & Executive Producer

Frank Abraham moved to California to earn a degree in Computer Science and never made it back home. He worked in the computer industry for companies including Apple Computer as a Strategic Alliance Manager and eventually for AT&T and various wireless companies as an independent computer contractor. "Out-of-the-blue one day, I decided to create a recipe sharing website" says Frank who has spent the last 3 years building his vision of *Cooking Hawaiian Style*. As people started taking notice and the site continued to grow, the concept of creating cooking videos for the web-site was born. The idea was to create more content for the website, not to start a cooking show that aired on TV. The notion of having a cooking show on TV seemed out of reach until he teamed up with Lanai Tabura.

LANAI TABURA
Host & Producer

Lanai Tabura is an accomplished radio disc jockey, actor, special event host and comedian. Sharing the namesake of his home town of Lāna'i, Lanai is a 20-year radio veteran, beginning his career in Honolulu with Clear Channel Radio. Lanai has interviewed some of the biggest names in Hollywood, including Paula Abdul, Queen Latifah, Dr. Dre, Easy E, Wayne Brady, Dr. Ruth, Mariah Carey, Boyz to Men, New Edition, and Snoop Dog among others. When he's not humoring listeners over the airwaves, Lanai has appeared in numerous TV shows, winner of The Food Network's *The Great Food Truck Race* season 4, *Anthonty Bourdaine, Diners, Drive Ins & Dives* and many commercials.